DESIGNING ARCHITECTURAL FACADES

an ideas file for architects

KURT HOFFMANN
HELGA GRIESE
WALTER MEYER-BOHE

GEORGE GODWIN LIMITED

*The book publishing subsidiary
of The Builder Group*

First published in German by Julius Hoffmann, Stuttgart 1973

This edition first published in Great Britain by
George Godwin Limited 1975

© For German-language edition, Julius Hoffmann, Stuttgart 1973

© For English-language translation, George Godwin Limited 1975

ISBN 0 7114 3408 5

George Godwin Limited
The book publishing subsidiary of
The Builder Group
2-4 Catherine Street
London WC2

Printed and bound in Great Britain by
Eyre & Spottiswoode Ltd
Thanet Press, Union Crescent, Margate

Designing Architectural Facades

Geno-Haus, Stuttgart, Bank and Administration Building of the Raiffeisen and Volksbanken Organisation

Architect: Hans Kammerer and Walter Belz, Stuttgart, in association with Ulrich Ziegler and Hans Röder

Reinforced concrete framed construction. Grid dimension 1.8 m, storey height 3.65 m. Precast concrete window sills with corbels for the maintenance access gallery. Windows fixed glazed with insulating glass. Anodised aluminium window frames and railings are dark bronze.

Window sill panes in pre-tensioned glass 8 mm thick, 207 cm high, 171 cm wide. The oversailing glass surfaces of the windows and balconies give the large building mass a light and weightless appearance.

Contents

Publisher's note

The usefulness and relevance of this work to the English-speaking market was such as to demand a translation, particularly since the German authors had selected a broad range of international examples of all types of facades.

As an ideas file the work of translation presented no problems, but since the book also offers hard technical information some reference has been made to German standards and to the availability of sizes for certain materials. A dagger has been used in the text where this may not be immediately apparent.†

In view of the range of countries which will use this English language edition, it has not been thought sensible to attempt to translate such data. The basic technical data from the German language edition has therefore been left. In many cases the data relevant to another country will be easily obtainable if not already known to the user of this book.

However for those interested in obtaining further information on particular German materials, DIN standards etc, the following addresses may be of use.

International Section
The Building Centre
26 Store Street
London WC1E 7BT
Tel: 01-636 1197
Carries a range of literature on overseas materials and products, including German, together with details of a number of agents in Britain.

British Standards Institution
2 Park Street
London W1A 2BS
Tel: 01-629 9000
The library carries all DIN standards which are available on loan to members. Copies can be purchased from the BSI sales department at the address below.

BSI Sales Department
101 Pentonville Road
London N1 9ND
Tel: 01-837 8801

American National Standards Institute
1430 Broadway
New York
New York 10018

American Society for Testing and Materials
PO Box 7510
Philadelphia
Pennsylvania 19101

Principles of construction

It is extremely difficult to lay down a systematic basis for the many possible types of wall constructions, ranging from traditional building work to light construction applied facades. However some sort of formal organisation is essential in a book: without it the book obviously does not work.

We have picked out three principles and have arranged this introduction and the examples that follow accordingly.

Solid walls: These are external walls with a continuous structural system, the load-bearing material of the facade being visible (eg, facing brickwork or exposed concrete) or directly covered (eg, rendering or mortar bedded tiles).

Rear ventilated cladding: Most cladding materials are not applied directly to the structural wall but are rear ventilated (not least on account of the imbalance of moisture vapour of the wall). These cladding materials range from shingles and slates, and light metal sheet, to large slab units anchored to the sub-structure.

Curtain walls: A curtain wall is essentially a light weight construction which is fixed to the sub-structure, either between light mullions or as edge-to-edge panels. Recent developments have resulted in the use of larger components including heavy precast concrete panels although these, by definition have no load-bearing function.

Scientific principles for building

Professor Hermann Reiher

Some points on building science for external wall construction

In the design and construction of external walls and facade elements, certain physical requirements must be satisfied in order that a healthy interior atmosphere is ensured, economical use of heating, ventilation and air conditioning is guaranteed, and deterioration of the building is avoided. The essential aspects of these provisions are drawn together in the standards: DIN 4108 'Thermal protection in Building Construction' and DIN 4109 'Noise Protection in Building Construction'.

In considering thermal and noise protection the relationship of wall to window should always be borne in mind. The smaller the proportion of solid wall, the less significant will be its physical characteristics in the total facade.

Fundamentals

Thermal protection and characteristics

From DIN 4108 'Thermal Protection in Building Construction'

Wall components

	Minimum thermal insulation figure $1/\Lambda$ Thermal insulation area		
	I	II	III
With wall weights 300 kp/m² the minimum thermal insulation figure $1/\Lambda$ (m² h C/kcal) should amount to	0.45	0.55	0.65
For light walls 300 kp/m² the insulation figure is to be increased to (about 20 kp/m²)	1.30	1.85	2.60

Table 1

Windows

A double glazed window offers at best only half the heat protection of a 36.5 cm thick brick wall. The following should therefore be considered for good thermal protection: at least two, or even better, three or four layers of air, external sunshade protection, and built-in joint sealants.

Thermal characteristics of the external skin in direct sunlight

It is necessary to avoid both damage caused by thermal stresses in the outer walls and overheating of the walls by taking precautions in the construction of the building. This includes choice of the right type and colour of materials, and use of rear ventilated external claddings, etc.

Tensional movements in metal constructions can cause disturbing noises.

Moisture protection

Walls have to be protected from rising damp from the ground. The external skin (rendering, paint, facing, applied skins etc) must prevent penetration of driving rain, whilst nevertheless allowing for movement of moisture vapour towards the external face of the building. For interior wall surfaces, rendering or paint is suitable for walls which allow a ready transmission of moisture vapour to the outside air. Laminated walls (sandwich panels) need a moisture vapour barrier close to the inside surface of the wall. 'Cold bridges' must be avoided.

Sound protection

From DIN 4109 'Sound Protection in Building Construction'

Walls should provide at least a 48 dB reduction.† In light walls horizontal transmissions must be avoided.

Windows. If a high reduction in noise is required, windows must be at least double glazed with variable thicknesses of glass, and with a minimum distance between panes of 7 cm.† In the space between, noise-absorbent materials should be placed on surfaces surrounding the window – ie, reveals, head and sill. Ventilation should be noise-reduced.

Local weather conditions

Consideration must be given to local climatic conditions for planning and construction. General data on wind, rain, sun, temperature and moisture, as well as information about specific climatic conditions are obtainable from meteorological offices. In high rise dwellings, which are subject to severe storms, special care must be given to protecting windows from wind and driving rain.

Healthy room climate

In areas where people work and rest the climatic conditions must promote well-being and good health. This will only be achieved if the external components of the building offer adequate protection against inclement weather (cold, heat, wind, rain etc) as well as protection from external noise sources. Rooms should also have efficient equipment for heating, ventilation and cooling adapted to external climatic conditions and internal climatic requirements.

The climate in rooms depends on a number of factors: the physical properties of the building and insulating materials, the size of windows, orientation of the building and rooms, the uses to which they are put, and the heating, ventilation and cooling systems. For an assessment of the quality of the climatic conditions of a room the following data is necessary:

Temperatures of the room air and surrounding wall surfaces (walls, ceiling and floor),

Moisture content of the air,

Air velocity,

Vertical temperature gradient (heat loss) of the room air,

Quality of the air (action of an aerosole and micro-organisms). As a rule, a comfortable, healthy room climate will be achieved if the following values are applied to the criteria listed above:

Temperatures

Critical temperature (average value of temperatures of the air and surfaces): in living rooms, offices and schools 19-21°C; in work rooms, depending on the intensity of the manual work, 12-19°C.

Floor temperatures: 20-24°C.

Maximum ceiling temperature (with ceiling radiation heating): ceiling heating surface 9-10 m²; average temperature according to room height – for 2.4 m, 3.0 m and 3.7 m: 28°C, 33°C, 40°C.

Relative humidity: 35-70%.

Air velocity around the occupants: <20 cm/sec.

Air conditions: Unpleasant concentrations of carbon dioxide, noxious materials, room dust, biological impurities and bacteria to be avoided.

In addition **noise** from the streets and neighbours to be excluded.

Minimum requirements for thermal, damp and noise protection

To guarantee acceptable climatic conditions in a room, certain minimum requirements for thermal, damp and noise protection must be satisfied, in particular for the external elements of the building. These are laid down in the appropriate standards – DIN 4108 'Thermal Protection in Building Construction', and DIN 4109 'Sound Protection in Building Construction'. These standards include, among other things, thermal insulation values $1/\Lambda$ for external walls and ceilings, and insulating values for airborne and structure-borne sound for walls and ceilings.†

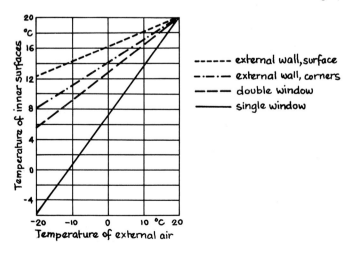

Figure 1. Range of temperatures of the inner surfaces of walls and windows not in direct sun and with a room temperature of 20°C, given a variety of external air temperatures

Minimum heat requirements

These are laid down according to DIN 4108 'Thermal Protection in Building Construction' $1/\Lambda$. If they are maintained in winter with continuous heating, the temperature of inner wall surfaces is then high enough to prevent condensation from forming on the walls, at least with normal household activities (air temperature 20°C, relative humidity not above 50%). For the three levels of thermal insulation I, II and III, laid down in Germany by DIN 4108, the thermal insulation values for heavy external building components (weight greater than 300 kg/m²) are as follows: 0.45, 0.55, 0.65 (m² h °C/kcal).†

These values only hold good for rooms with continuous heating. In conditions of periodic heating, a higher thermal capacity or special insulating precautions are necessary. In **lightweight external walls** higher levels of thermal insulation must always be applied, as shown below, since such walls have a low storage capacity.

Weight of the building component in kp/m²	Thermal insulation value $1/\Lambda$ (m² h °C/kcal) for various thermal insulation levels		
	I	II	III
20	1.30	1.85	2.60
50	1.00	1.40	2.00
100	0.70	0.95	1.30
150	0.55	0.65	0.90
200	0.50	0.60	0.75
300	0.45	0.55	0.65

Table 2. Minimum thermal insulation value $1/\Lambda$ for light external walls (weight under 300 kp/m²) according to DIN 4108†

Lightweight external walls which are subject to intensive sunlight should be protected on the outside with a rear ventilated protective skin, similar to the so-called 'cold roof', to reflect the sun's rays so that the walls do not heat up too much in summer. (See also page 108).

The **windows** require special consideration as an inherent part of the external surface of a building because of their effect on climatic room conditions and running costs. Provided they are not directly exposed to the sun's rays, the inner surface of single or double glazed windows have a temperature less than that of an external wall, thermally insulated to standard specification (Figure 1). Only with two sealed air spaces (three panes, in other words) and air-tight installation will the thermal insulation of the window surface actually correspond to the adjoining wall components. Conversely in winter on the sunny side of the building, the sun's rays falling on the glass surfaces can provide a noticeable heat gain. All the same in summer the sun's rays can become a nuisance, because they themselves heat the contents of the room (air, furniture and building elements). In addition, when they pass through the windows, the glass surfaces absorb the heat (for south-facing windows in July, up to 4°C – see Figure 2) and so act as overheated, large-surface convectors. To ensure optimum environmental efficiency for windows which are placed in walls subject to direct sunlight it is necessary to provide suitable sun protection appliances, fixed to the outside of the window. In many cases a glass with stronger reflective action will serve (see page 24).

With movable windows the **joints** must be well sealed. With normal window arrangements, heat loss occurs for the main part through the joints, especially in windy conditions. Inadequately sealed window grooves, for example, can reduce the thermal protection of a double glazed window to that of a single glazed window. In order to obtain the most effective and durable

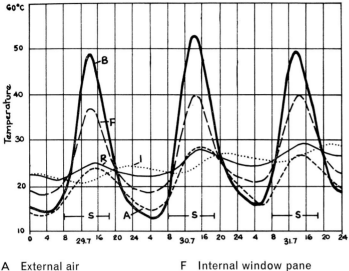

A External air
B External window panel
S Period for which window receives sunshine
F Internal window pane
I Internal plaster of the window panel
R Room air

Figure 2. Penetration of sun in summer through large window facing south, and the effect of the external temperature and sunlight on the temperature of the wall, window panel, internal glass pane and room air (Munich 29-31 July 1960)

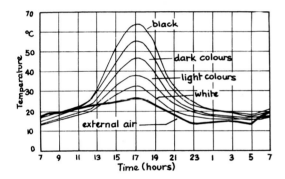

Figure 3. Effect of colour on the temperature of the upper surface of the external rendering of a west wall (30 cm pumice block walling) measured on 5 July 1959 (radiation on horizontal surface 660 gcal/cm² day)

With all countries in the temperate zone of the earth endeavouring to conserve energy, it is particularly significant that approximately one third of the total present day energy consumption is used for air conditioning and heating of buildings. Mainly for this reason, as well as in order to ensure healthy room conditions and to reduce the amount of fumes from heating appliances, most countries are striving to raise the standard of insulation in external wall construction and by so doing improve living conditions. Recent developments in production and refinement of building and insulating materials provide us with the means to achieve this. The examples given in Figures

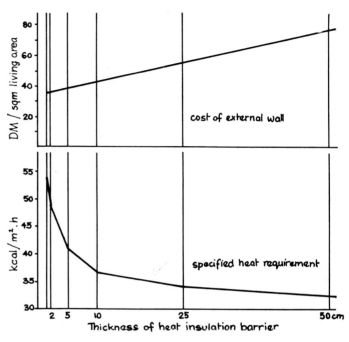

Figure 4. Building costs and heat requirements of buildings with multi-layer walls and various thicknesses of heat insulation. Optimum thickness of the heat insulation layer approx. 10 cm (from W. Triebel, *The Economic Advantages of Structural Heat Protection*, 1964)

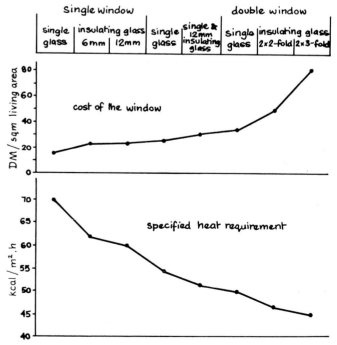

Figure 5. Cost of various types of window, and the heat requirements of buildings with these windows (from W. Triebel, see Figure 4)

joint seals, new windows are increasingly being supplied already fitted with a special sealing device (eg, spring clips of non-corrosive metal, or weather-resistant and permanently resilient plastics).

The **external walls** of a building warmed by the **sun's rays,** and the increase in temperature of the external surface and outer layers of the wall depends, in the first instance, on the colour of the wall surface and on the degree of heat absorption of the external material $b = \sqrt{c \lambda y}$ (kcal m²h½grd) .Temperature variants were measured on a cloudless summer day for the west side of a building with 30 cm pumice block/brickwork walls (see Figure 3). Whilst the white surfaces warmed up to only slightly above the air temperature, on the immediately adjoining black surfaces the temperature rose to over 60°C. The various temperatures of the coloured surfaces were somewhere between these two values.

Such large temperature variations can result in tension variations eventually leading to structural damage, eg, large or small areas of rendering soon becoming unkeyed from the substructure.

| | | | Mid-winter minima | | | | |
			−10°	−15°	−20°	−25°	−30°
Germany	DIN 4108	MW	0.45	0.55	0.65	—	—
	Proposed by L. Sautter	VW c	0.80	1.00	1.20	1.40	1.60
		VW b	1.25	1.50	1.75	2.00	2.25
		VW a	1.70	2.00	2.30	2.60	2.90
Austria	'O' standard I	MW	—	0.57	0.68	0.79	0.89
	B 8110 II	VW c	—	0.86	1.02	1.19	1.34
	III	VW b	—	1.14	1.36	1.58	1.78
	IV	VW a	—	1.71	2.04	2.37	2.67
Denmark	Housing Ministry	MW	0.70	0.70	—	—	—
	Building Research Institute	VW	2.00	2.00	—	—	—
Norway	Building Research Institute	brick walls	—	0.70	0.80	0.90	1.05
		other walls	—	0.80	0.90	1.05	1.25
Sweden	Building Regulations	brick walls	—	0.70	0.80	0.90	1.05
		other walls	—	1.05	1.25	1.25	1.50
England	Regulations for heating of buildings		1.15	1.15	1.15	1.15	1.15
Italy	Proposed by G. Massari		0.80	0.80	1.00	1.00	1.00

Table 3. Proposals for total thermal protection of heavy external walls (weight at least 300 kg/m²). The numbers represent thermal insulation values $1/\varLambda$ in m² h grd/kcal. MW = minimum thermal protection, VW = full thermal protection (source: L. Sautter)

| | | | | Mid-winter minima | | | | |
				−10°	−15°	−20°	−25°	−30°
≥200 kg/m²	Germany	DIN 4108	MW	0.50	0.60	0.75	—	—
		Proposed by	VW c	0.85	1.10	1.30	1.50	1.70
		L. Sautter	VW b	1.30	1.60	1.90	2.20	2.50
			VW a	1.75	2.10	2.50	2.90	3.30
≥150 kg/m²	Germany	DIN 4108	MW	0.55	0.65	0.90	—	—
		Proposed by	VW c	1.00	1.20	1.50	1.80	2.10
		L. Sautter	VW b	1.40	1.75	2.15	2.55	2.95
			VW a	1.80	2.30	2.80	3.30	3.60
	Denmark	Housing Ministry	MW	1.00	1.00	—	—	—
	Norway	Building Research Institute	MW	—	0.90	1.05	1.25	1.50
≥100 kg/m²	Germany	DIN 4108	MW	0.70	0.95	1.30	—	—
		Proposed by	VW c	1.20	1.50	1.90	2.30	2.70
		L. Sautter	VW b	1.60	2.10	2.60	3.10	3.60
			VW a	2.00	2.70	3.40	3.90	4.50
	Denmark	Housing Ministry	MW	—	1.00	1.00	—	—
	Sweden	Building Regulations	MW	—	1.80	1.80	2.30	2.30
≥50 kg/m²	Germany	DIN 4108	MW	1.00	1.40	1.90	—	—
		Proposed by	VW c	1.50	2.00	2.60	3.20	—
		L. Sautter	VW b	1.90	2.60	3.40	4.20	—
			VW a	2.30	3.20	4.20	5.00	—
	Denmark	Housing Ministry	MW	—	1.80	1.80	—	—
≥20 kg/m²	Germany	DIN 4108	MW	1 30	1.85	2.60	—	—
		Proposed by	VW c	1.80	2.50	3.40	—	—
		L. Sautter	VW b	2.20	3.10	4.30	—	—
			VW a	2.60	3.70	5.20	—	—
	Denmark	Housing Ministry	MW	—	1.80	1.80	—	—

Table 4. Proposals for total thermal protection for light external walls (weight under 300 kg/m²) (source: L. Sautter)

4 and 5 show what considerable savings can be made by **optimum thermal protection** of walls and windows. Recently in various countries in Europe (Austria, Denmark, Norway, Sweden, Poland, Czechoslovakia, Italy, England and others), the standards laid down by building regulations for thermal insulation in building construction have been revised in order to improve living standards and to save costs. Other countries have indicated that this will be done. Suggested standards for external walls are shown in Tables 3 and 4.

It goes without saying that more effective thermal protection improves living conditions and has real economic advantages. The following two examples show this.

Take a single-family house (450 m³ of space, open situation, normal wind conditions, thermal insulation – range III) and compare total costs – including cost of building – first for normal and then full thermal insulation. The results are shown in Table 5.

With full thermal insulation significant savings are apparent when the building has been in use for a period of five years or more.

		Results from following DIN 4108	in %	Results with full thermal protection	in %
A	Total heat loss of the building	17 250 kcal	100	8 150 kcal	47.2
B	Building costs without heating plant	53 800,—DM	100	57 360,—DM	106.6
C	Cost of heating plant (DM 0.02/kcal)	3 450,—DM	100	1 630,—DM	47.2
D	Total building costs (B + C)	57 250,—DM	100	58 990,—DM	103
E	Heating oil requirements/Heat period (0.24 kcal)	4 140 1/Yr.	100	1 956,—1/Yr.	47.2
F	Heating oil requirements/ Heat period (DM 162,—/100 l)	671,—DM/Yr.	100	317,—DM/Yr.	47.2
G	Building and heating costs in 5 years (5 × F) + D	60 605,—DM/5 Yr.	100	60 575,—DM/5 Yr.	99.9
H	Building and heating costs in 25 years (25 × F) + D	74 025,—DM/25 Yr.	100	66 915,—DM/25 Yr.	90.4
J	Building and heating costs in 50 years (50 × F) + D	90 800,—DM/50 Yr.	100	74 480,—DM/50 Yr.	82.4

Table 5. Comparative costs for normal and full thermal insulation, based on a single-family house with 450 m³ of space, two-thirds of ground floor over cellars, open situation, normal wind conditions, thermal insulation – range III (from H. Schmidt) *Publisher's note:* To avoid confusion currency figures have not been converted.

Experience with multi-family buildings shows that improved thermal insulation can be achieved for an extra building cost of only 1.5 to 3.0%, and the heat consumption is then reduced by 15-30%. In addition, there are improved climatic conditions in the rooms, resulting from higher surface temperatures of walls and windows. Optimum thermal insulation of all external building elements – walls, windows, floors and roof – as is being achieved to an increasing extent abroad, inevitably produces fundamental economic advantages, as is shown in Table 6.

With larger buildings it is not sufficient simply to follow letter for letter the scientifically determined thermal insulation values required in DIN 4108. The following example shows why this is so.

In a block of flats consisting of three four-storey two-span buildings, the specified thermal requirements of the various flats were in the ratio 1:1:6. For the flats in the middle of the block, this came to 29.2 kcal/h m³, and for the flats at the ends of the block 39.3 kcal/h m³. These exposed flats, especially those at the end of the top floors, are responsible for dispersing heat energy and require even further thermal insulation in the external building elements.

Scientifically determined requirements for damp protection

Excessive dampness in building materials reduces their thermal insulation properties. This leads to an unhealthy room environment (among other things, mildew fungus on damp surfaces) and to the destruction of building materials by frost action, decomposition, or the action of biological building pests (vermin, fungi, dry rot, bacteria etc) which flourish in damp conditions. It also leads to allergies and disease among the inhabitants, especially children. Once the drying out of a new building is complete, the main sources of dampness are,

externally, from driving rain and, internally, from moisture in the air produced during use. The external components must therefore be protected as much as possible from these sources of dampness.

The **damp absorption** of a rendered external wall during storms depends firstly on the capilliary action of the external rendering and, over a longer period, on its permeability and on the degree of water absorption of the walling materials.

The water repellent characteristics of the external rendering (eg, coatings or paint) deserve particular attention. During the initial drying out process the moisture in the rendering will evaporate. **Subsequent drying out** will be regulated by the speed at which the moisture in the rendering adjacent to the wall surface moves towards the outer surface of the rendering by capilliary action, and then evaporates. The greater the capilliary absorption of the wall material, the quicker the wall will dry out. When the wall cannot fulfil this compensating process, as with clinker and light curtain walls, special attention must be paid to the effects of driving rain on the wall.

The warmer the air, the more moisture it can absorb. 1 kg of air (approx. 1 m³) at 0°C absorbs approx. 4 g of water; at 25°C approx. 20 g (**absolute humidity**). The **relative humidity** gives the percentage of water actually held by the air in relation to its maximum retention capacity.

1 kg of air with a 50% relative humidity and temperature of 20°C contains 10 g of water. When this air cools down to 0°C 6 g of water will condense since the air cannot hold more than 4 g/kg at which point it becomes saturated.

The result is that **moisture is absorbed** from the air since there is an imbalance of water vapour in the atmosphere due to the fall in water vapour pressure together with the varying resistance to diffusion in and through the walls from the warmer to the colder side. Because of the greater moisture retention capacity of materials used in traditional wall construction (eg, normal rendered walls of clay brick, sand lime brick or pumice concrete), an increase in the moisture content of the wall, as a result of underestimating the saturation temperature, and the consequent reduction in thermal protection are not significant. However this is not the case with lightweight types of wall construction that consist mainly of layers of varying building materials with relatively less moisture capacity.

Here the rule must be that the water vapour permeability of the wall layers must increase progressively from interior to exterior so that water vapour can succeed in reaching the outer surface without hindrance. On the other hand, the levelling out of moisture vapour will be checked or retarded by an external wall whose surface is damp proofed on the outside but not on the inside. Only where rooms are constantly heated, with a relative humidity of less than 45%, and with walls subject to direct sunshine on the outside, can walls of greater capillarity

and with damp proofing on the outer surface be assumed to be trouble-free in constantly wet conditions.

Moisture levels in walls and roof will be considerably affected by the sun, and because the interior temperature will fall below that of the exterior of the building, moisture will then move from the wall back into the room atmosphere.

Flat roofs and walls exposed to the sun therefore have a greater capacity for drying out than was hitherto generally believed.

Scientifically determined requirements for sound protection

The degree of sound insulation necessary for the external construction of a house is governed principally by the noise penetration from traffic and from inhabitants in neighbouring buildings.

	External wall		Floor (ground storey)	
	uninsulated	well insulated	uninsulated	well insulated
Thermal conductivity kcal/m² °C h	k = 1.2	k = 0.3	k = 1.8	k = 0.5
Intermediate value kcal/m² °C h per day	24 × 1.2 = 28.8	24 × 0.3 = 7.2	24 × 1.8 = 43.2	24 × 0.5 = 12
Theoretical heat loss per m² per year (over 3 000 heat grade days) kcal/m² per year	28.8 × 3000 = 86 400	7.2 × 3000 = 21 600	43.2 × 3000 = 129 600	12 × 3000 = 36 000
Theoretical loss per m² per year kWh/m² per year	$\frac{86\,400}{860} = 100$	$\frac{21\,600}{860} = 25$	$\frac{129\,600}{860} = 151$	$\frac{36\,000}{860} = 42$
Actual loss per m² per year (temperature reduction etc,) kWh/m² per year	$\frac{14}{24} \cdot 100 = 58.6$	$\frac{14}{24} \cdot 25 = 15$	$\frac{14}{24} \cdot 151 = 88$	$\frac{14}{24} \cdot 42 = 24$
Annual cost in DM/m² per year (tariff 5Pf/kWh)	58.6 × 0.05 = 2.94	15 × 0.05 = 0.75	88 × 0.05 = 4.38	24 × 0.05 = 1.20
Additional cost of insulation material including fixing DM m²	—	ca. 10,—	—	ca. 13.50
Annual saving through additional insulation DM m²	—	2.19	—	3.18

	Roof		Glazing	
	uninsulated	well insulated	single	double
Thermal conductivity kcal/m² °C h	k = 1.8	k = 0.3	k = 5	k = 2.7
Intermediate value kcal/m² °C h per day	24 × 1.8 = 43.2	24 × 0.3 = 7.2	24 × 5 = 120	24 × 2.7 = 64.8
Theoretical heat loss per m² per year (over 3000 heat grade days) kcal/m² per year	43.2 × 3000 = 129 600	7.2 × 3000 = 21 600	120 × 3000 = 360 000	64.8 × 3000 = 194 400
Theoretical loss per m² per year kWh/m² per year	$\frac{129\,500}{860} = 151$	$\frac{21\,600}{860} = 25$	$\frac{360\,000}{860} = 420$	$\frac{194\,400}{860} = 226$
Actual loss per m² per year (temperature reduction etc,) kWh/m² per year	$\frac{14}{24} \cdot 151 = 88$	$\frac{14}{24} \cdot 25 = 15$	$\frac{14}{24} \cdot 420 = 240$	$\frac{14}{24} \cdot 226 = 132$
Annual cost in DM/m² per year (tariff 5Pf/kWh)	88 × 0.05 = 4.38	15 × 0.05 = 0.75	240 × 0.05 = 12,—	132 × 0.05 = 6.60
Additional cost of insulation material including fixing DM m²	—	ca. 16,—	—	ca. 63,—
Annual saving through additional insulation DM m²	—	3.63	—	5.40

Table 6. Economics of thermal insulation in multi-family buildings (from P. Borstelmann)

Publisher's note: To avoid confusion currency figures have not been converted.

Room type	Situation	Sound level with closed windows (phons)			
		day		night	
		desired level†	limit*	desired level†	limit*
living, rest, recreation rooms with general functions	quiet situation, noise insulated areas, residential areas	25	35	20	25
	mixed areas, urban areas	35	45	25	35
	industrial areas	40	50	30	40

		desired level	limit
hospital wards, film radio recording rooms		25	30
school rooms, reading rooms, lecture theatres, concert and theatre halls, offices		30	40
stores, assembly rooms, quiet restaurants		35	45
large restaurants, typing pools		45	55

*Maximum levels to be required until further empirical values are established

Table 7. Noise disturbance levels in rooms with closed windows (partly taken from F. Bruckmayer)

Basically noise protection is determined by the sound protection offered by the **windows** which on average is about 20/30 dB below the noise insulation standard for external walls (except in the case of extremely light wall skins). For this reason it is pointless to expect the level of sound protection in external walls to be higher than about 48 dB. On the other hand it is necessary to determine which type of window construction would enable the noise of traffic (75/85 dB) to be reduced to an acceptable level of 25/40 dB (see Table 7).† With a single glazed airtight window, with 3 mm glass panes, a sound insulation measurement of around 25 dB is attained. With a thickness of 9 mm, 30 dB, using double glazed windows with varying thicknesses of glass reduction values of 35/40 dB can be achieved, provided the following requirements are met. Firstly, if the panes are kept at a distance of more than 75 mm from one another; secondly if the inner surfaces are treated with sound absorbing materials; and thirdly if sound-insulated ventilation devices are installed so that the windows need not be opened except for cleaning.

When looking at the **total sound protection** of a building, we must give separate consideration to the individual parts of the total sound field. These include the sound transmitted from room to room by vibration of walls and ceilings, and the longitudinal transmission of sound through and along stiff, thin building components such as load-bearing thin walls, light ceilings etc. These longitudinal transmissions are in many cases greater than the direct sound transmissions from room to room through wall or ceiling. For this reason the reduction requirements between adjoining rooms are not achieved simply by constructing walls and ceilings to standards derived from building regulations. Thus, for example, a continuous curtain wall carried on timber framing can transmit intensified noise from one dwelling to another more readily than the adequately insulated walls and ceiling which support it. These longitudinal transmissions can be eliminated by making such cladding discontinuous, and by supporting it on stiff columns and beams (see Figure 6).

The disturbance from noise caused by **water-borne transmission** can be reduced, and even eliminated, by building in noise-reducing mountings for taps and valves, and adopting the guiding principles set down in the supplement to DIN 4109 'Noise Protection in Building Construction – Mountings and Apparatus for Water Systems'.

Local weather conditions

Included in the building regulations and codes of practice for most countries are simple rules for the protection of occupants against cold, heat, wind and rain. For the planning and future use of industrial and residential areas, however, climatic data must be gathered together and grouped in a practical and usable way, with information on sunshine, temperatures, air humidity, wind rates and rainfall (average values and variations).

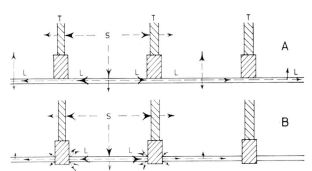

A The longitudinal transmission L acts like an attenuated sound absorber for the separating walls T
B The abutment points absorb the longitudinal transmissions
S Sound source

Figure 6. Schematic representation of the action of longitudinal noise transmission in thin, stiff curtain walls

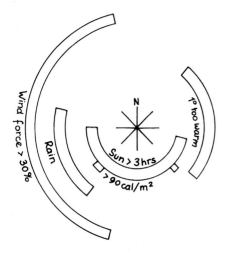

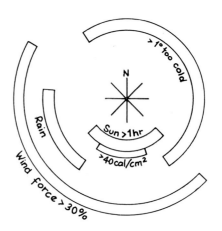

SUMMER
Sunshine: from ESE to W walls more than 3 hours daily, direct radiation 90 cal/cm²
Wind force on SSW and NNW walls more than 30% of the time over 3 Beaufort
Rain: SW and WNW walls
Wind: NE and SE winds; as a result of warm air, an increase in the mid temperatures of approx. 1°C

Table 12. Climatic data for building: Influence of weather factors on a building in Hamburg (according to Reidat, Ocean Weather Observatory)

WINTER
Sunshine: longer than 1 hour daily on SE to SW walls, direct radiation over 40 cal/cm²
Wind force on SE to NW walls for more than 30% of the time winds over 3 Beaufort
Rain: SW and W walls
Wind: NW and SE winds causing cooling off of more than 1°C

In order to have available continuous and accurate local weather data, in many cities (eg London, Paris, Vienna, Hamburg, Belgrade) the amount of climatic data collected for the whole region (including noise and air pollution) far exceeds the normal day-to-day measurements. The aim of this is to provide climatic data for building purposes.

An example of the use of such data for the purposes of building is given in Figure 7 and is from the Hamburg Weather Observatory.

Solar protection

As mentioned in the section on building science, the direct radiation from the sun can, in certain circumstances, affect considerably the heat balance of the building. Long periods of sunshine on windows in winter produce a noticeable heat gain; conversely in summer this continuous radiation can cause extreme overheating of the rooms.

In houses with complete air conditioning, it is possible that the energy required in the summer for cooling purposes will be much greater than that required for heating in the winter.

When the window area is shaded by means of a fixed blind (as illustrated on pages 115, 119), by roof eaves (as on pages 34, 78, 161), by balconies (as on pages 54, 88) or by another facade component (as on pages 59, 107, 113, 148, 149) careful consideration should be given to the meridian angles of the sun throughout the course of the year, and the areas of radiation affecting the building, bearing in mind the orientation and the time of day.

In order to obtain the best effect from movable blinds they can be motorised or of fully automatic design. The various types of solar protection are most effective when fixed on the outside of the window; the radiation energy is thereby dissipated before it has penetrated through the window panes. Protection at night or in winter can be achieved by reversing the process and placing the blind on the inside. Both these processes are possible by using pivot windows with louvres or venetian blinds (eg, page 137).

Fire protection

Building regulations lay down rules for external wall construction in general terms, and special requirements can be made for walls built of combustible materials. In external walls these may be devices for fixing fire brigade ladders or the construction of staircases for fire escape, etc.

In high buildings the most important precaution is to prevent the spread of fire from one storey to another. A path of resistance to flame-spread must be provided not less than 1 m wide at every floor level, and all columns and beams must be fire resistant.

For this purpose 10 cm concrete, 11.5 cm brickwork, 8 cm plaster are sufficient.†

With any unusual facade construction, especially in the case of high buildings, it is recommended that the proposals are discussed with the appropriate fire authority at the earliest possible stages of planning.

The behaviour of building materials in the facade

The **sun** can heat up a wall surface to over 60°C (in extreme cases to above 100°C). In central Europe it can also be as cold as −30°C.

Temperature differences can cause a longitudinal increase in an aluminium sheet of 11 mm in 5 m, and of 40 mm in a PVC sheet. On the inside of the building the temperature/dimensional relationship is stable.

Radiation from the sun, especially the ultra violet rays, can cause some plastics to become brittle due to the evaporation of the plasticisers. With an increasingly polluted atmosphere, dust is deposited on surfaces which, when combined with water, becomes chemically active.

The sulphuric acid content can stain or even destroy natural stone, it also attacks renderings.

In many cities an additional nuisance are bird droppings, which are not only unpleasant but can cause considerable damage to buildings.

In districts with a high soot content in the atmosphere, it is not only necessary to consider how the building will look in 5, 10 or 50 years, but whether and by what means the exterior surfaces of the building will have to be cleaned, in particular the windows and large areas of glass.

Rainwater contributes to pollution and resultant weathering problems. Only horizontal surfaces are washed clean and the dirt is carried down over the facade, causing dark staining from the soot content and white stones on limestone because of its conversion to gypsum (calcium sulphate) in sulphuric acid atmospheres.

An early example of an architect's solution to this problem is Marcel Breuer's 'Bijenkorf' in Rotterdam. Breuer designed the limestone slabs to be fixed at various angles, the weathering patterns emphasising the slab structure.

Another possibility is to allow rainwater to run off behind the facade (see page 107) or to channel it away to some extent (see page 150). For an example of damage resulting from damp penetration, see page 13.

The construction of an external wall and its cross section, therefore, should not be seen merely from the aesthetic viewpoint but must also come to terms with the practical problems.

Quite apart from the cost of construction, consideration must also be given to the cost of **maintaining and cleaning** the building. Just as **heating costs** have to be reckoned in terms of the thermal insulation of the external walls, so, too, with air-conditioned buildings the cooling costs have to be taken into account when assessing the overall running costs of the building. Here are a few indications:

	Thermal insulation	Costs
1 sq m of wall (38 cm brickwork with rendering)	100%	100%
1 sq m of window (timber with insulating glass)	30%	200%
1 sq m window sill area of curtain wall	100%	400%

Table 8

Consideration should also be given to the question of **repair costs.** For example, can the paint selected be renewed quite simply after the appropriate time, and are there problems over replacing glass or facade panels when breakages occur?

The reduction in strength of curtain walls, as against solid walls, increases the useful surface area. With a reduction in wall thickness of 20 cm and a base construction surface area of 15 × 25 m, this gain is around 5%.

There are inherent problems in the use of building materials, construction and working processes which, although well established and satisfactory in one area, may behave quite differently in other climates, even if one employs a specialist firm from the original area. For example, clinker walls are a firmly established technique in North Germany, but give rise to problems in South Germany because the masons there lack the necessary technical knowledge.

In **tall buildings** wind speeds must be borne in mind, as they exercise pressure and suction in increasing strengths and may even drive the rain vertically upwards.

Solid walls
Facing brickwork

Hard burnt bricks and clinker are frost resistant, clinker being more so because, in burning, the high temperature causes incipient fusing to take place. The bricks are very dense and have almost no moisture absorption.

Hard burned brick is the most suitable for facing work. With hard burnt bricks as with rendering, moisture that is absorbed in the wall will evaporate from the entire surface. With clinker, however, this is restricted to the surface area of the joints.

For facing brickwork to look good, the bricks must be square and of uniform dimensions, and not break easily.

A recent development is the 'capilliary brick', made from dry pressed reconstructed stone, which is claimed to have the advantage of being moisture-resistant. These bricks can also be supplied with a silicone impregnation on four sides. From Holland a brick is obtainable having a white glaze fused onto the face side.

Facing brickwork requires careful construction, no damaged bricks should be used, and bed and vertical joints should be properly filled with mortar. Only free-standing scaffolding should be used and no ties taken into the brickwork. Surfaces must be protected against staining.

Frost retarders should not be used in the mortar because of the risk of efflorescence. Expansion joints must be provided at approx. 8-12 m.†

Single skin brickwork

Common bricks are suitable for use in walls which are to be rendered but not for facing brickwork, for which the external skin should be of hard burnt bricks or clinker, properly bonded to the inner skin of the wall. The total cross section of the wall can be statically stressed, and in calculating the thermal resistivity the total wall thickness must be considered.

Despite the popularity of hard burned bricks, solid brickwork often proves more economical these days since, unlike cavity brickwork, it can be erected in one operation. The brickwork must be constructed so that any moisture that is absorbed can evaporate from the whole cross section of the wall to the external air.

The joints should be capable of absorbing and evaporating water but the faced surfaces, especially on the prevailing weather side, should not be too absorbent in walls of ≦36.5 cm thickness.†

The **bed mortar** should adhere firmly and should be of adequate thickness and filled into all the joints. English and Flemish bonds are the best. The internal joints in the bond should not be less than 2 cm since they act as moisture impeders, as do the joints on the outer surface of the wall.†

If **clinker** is built into the outer surface of the wall, the jointing mortar must be absolutely dense and water repellent.

In all cases uncracked bricks should be used. Particular care should be taken to ensure that all butt joints are properly filled.

With recessed or undercut joints, spalling of the bricks can occur because of frost action.

The joints should be raked 2 cm deep (preferably with a scoring stick), the joints cleaned of loose mortar and carefully pointed with a suitable pointing mortar.†

A mortar mix consisting of 1 part Portland cement to 3 parts of well graded sand 0-2 mm, properly mixed to a good consistency, has proved satisfactory.

Mortar which is used too dry can weather badly.

Two skin brickwork

In two skin walling, with or without a cavity, the external skin should not be load bearing and should be supported at every floor level. A floor slab that is not insulated acts as a 'cold bridge'.

Joints between all wall skins, and overlying concrete tie rods, should only be filled with permanently resilient mastic. For further details on joints, see page 22. If special strengthening precautions are provided for, the external skin of a cavity wall can be carried up to eight storeys without cavity ties; but generally the height of external skins of cavity walls is restricted to two storeys. Otherwise there may be difficulties due to wind loading, variable thermal expansion movements in the inner and outer skins, and the removal of condensation moisture.†

Facing brickwork without a cavity

In these walls the bonding is not continuous, and only the inner skin of the wall should be taken into account in structural calculations. Thermal insulation will be effective over the total wall thickness. If the inner skin of the wall is unable to take up the anticipated rainfall (especially in thin walls with weak bond and where rainfall is heavy) a dense insulating layer can be placed between the two skins (eg, a cement mortar layer of 1:3 mix with a water-proof additive) so that the external skin becomes completely saturated. The total joint thickness should be 2-2.5 cm.†

The external skin of the wall can be built up afterwards. If this is done during good weather staining can be avoided.

Facing brickwork with a cavity

The external skin is intended to give protection from rain penetration and should not be loadbearing. Thermal insulation is effective over the total wall thickness. The cavity should be 6-7 cm wide and ventilated at the top and bottom (in 20 m² of wall surface, about 150 m² of abutment joints should be left open). Where the inner and outer skins are in contact (base, wall openings, supports), they must be separated with a layer of 500-grade building paper. The skins are tied together with galvanised steel ties (at least 5 ties per square metre), separated by distances of 30 cm vertically and 75 cm horizontally. These should not be exceeded.† An insulation layer on the inner wall facing the cavity is to be recommended. Thermal insulation is then on the cold side of the wall protected from the rain, and provides a good diffusion barrier.

Sand lime bricks

These are made from quartz sand and lime and are cured in an autoclave process. Sand lime bricks with a crushing strength of 150 kp/cm² and 250 kp/cm² are frost resistant and may be used in facing brickwork.

The combination of sand lime bricks for the outer skin and a high porosity brick for the inner skin is considered to be quite good.

Quarried stone

Quarried stone has a good thermal conductivity and therefore walls of quarried stone almost always need additional thermal insulation. At the base of a building stones should only be laid parallel to their split edge. The jointing mortar should be of the same density as the stone (cement mortar should not be used with soft stones).

Paint protection on concrete and brickwork

The extent to which paints can prevent water from penetrating a wall depends on their composition and thickness, conversely, as with thick renderings, they can delay the diffusion of moisture in the wall from inside to outside, causing a build-up of moisture behind the paint film which is finally forced off. For this reason film-forming paints should not be used and only those which can 'breathe' are recommended.

Brickwork is frequently treated with **colourless silicone resin coatings.** These act by allowing rainwater to cling only in droplets. Evaporation of moisture is not delayed and the wall has enhanced weathering properties since particles of dirt are not attached to the actual surface.

With silicone treatments it is necessary to differentiate between water soluble silicones and silicone resin in an organic solution.

The application of silicones should only be entrusted to established firms as the coating is colourless and the in-experienced workman may apply uneven coats which may appear patchy in rain.

The coating should only be applied to walls where the mortar has properly set as fresh mortar or concrete attack silicones which, when used as a waterproofer, can combine with free lime.

A good silicone coating will last for 6-7 years. Before renewal the walls should be thoroughly cleaned with fresh water, as should old facades before a first treatment.

Paints with a **mineral base** are suitable for brickwork but it is necessary to ensure that the mortar has set hard before dispersion paints are applied. Coats should be applied thinly and evenly. Oil-based paints are unsuitable for use on concrete and renderings (sealing film).

For **whitening** a paint made from white lime (and in certain circumstances with an amount of white cement added) may be applied in two or three coats. An amount of fine sharp river sand can be added and this will help evaporation of moisture from the wall and make the coating correspondingly thicker.

For areas of high rainfall whitening is not suitable and a thin rendering is preferable. This may be finished with a dispersion paint. The job of whitening or painting brickwork must be carried out with as much preparation and care as for facing brickwork.

External renderings today are almost exclusively ready-mixed preparations. Those renderings which are actually thrown onto the surface (pebbledash, spatterdash, Tyrolean renderings) are generally better than those which are applied and surfaced by rubbing with a trowel. This causes cement laitence to be brought to the surface and this in turn leads to fine surface cracking of the rendering.

Exposed insitu concrete

Exposed insitu concrete is concrete with a pre-determined surface finish. Generally it shows the texture of the formwork but the surface can also be treated as exposed concrete aggregate, sandblasted or hand-dressed by a mason. Subsequent patching or repairing invariably remains visible and surface faults are better left alone.

It is advisable to have test surfaces cast and ensure that the specialist firm doing the work indemnifies against subsequent defective work.

If there is any doubt about matters such as vibration times, additives and so on specialist contractors should be consulted. Even when it is not actually necessary, B300 or a higher grade should be specified for exposed concrete work.

The **colour** of the exposed concrete is mainly dependent upon the colour of the cement, and to a lesser extent upon the fine aggregate content. The type of cement and the delivery sequence should be maintained throughout the course of the work. To a lesser extent, this also applies to the coarse and fine aggregates. For white concrete, white cement and white sand is used, and by adding coloured alkali-resistant pigments, coloured concretes can be achieved to some extent.

Formwork must be individually designed (outer surface, board widths, formwork direction, board abutments, lining sheets, etc). This applies especially to all details and junctions, slots and chases for installations. For highly complex work, study models may be necessary to scales of 1:50, 1:10, even full-scale mock-ups may be needed.

Construction (or daywork) joints should not be obstrusive in the completed wall and are best formed, for example, in shaded grooves.

Tension wires are drawn through plastic 'guides' which hardly mark the concrete surface and can be withdrawn with the shuttering. Heavy formwork requires a moderate amount of joinery work to prevent the cement laitence (slurry) from running out of the joints. The shuttering must also be kept damp.

In order to **texture** the surface of the concrete, the formwork can be lined with factory-made, impressed sheets of foamed plastic (eg, polystyrene) or rigid PVC (see page 56).

Individual shapes, which may also be used for precast concrete components, can be made from GRP (glass reinforced plastic) polyester (see page 115).

The reinforcement must be adequately covered by the concrete to avoid rust stains, and where exposed to the open air must be at least 20 mm thick and at least 5 mm greater than the largest size of aggregate used in the concrete.† This is necessary to avoid 'honeycombing' on the surface during the pouring process.

The **thermal conductivity** of concrete (even dense concrete with a density 1.9 to 2.5 kp/dm³) is around 2½ times greater than that of brickwork. Generally therefore, it is necessary to add extra thermal insulation which can be provided on the internal wall surface or within the wall thickness. In the latter case, insulation must not be used which will impede the diffusion of moisture through the wall. A suitable material is expanded polystyrene board; however care should be taken that it is not damaged whilst the concrete is applied and consolidated.

Lightweight concrete (density below 1.8 kp/dm³) has high thermal insulation. Foamed concrete (G525) is a better insulator than brickwork. By using lightweight aggregates such as natural pumice or blast furnace slag, a lightweight concrete with good thermal properties can also be achieved. Expanded clay aggregates (eg, leca) absorb hardly any moisture and produce a high-strength concrete with excellent thermal insulation properties.

Lightweight concretes may be reinforced or unreinforced for moulded components, large size blocks or panels. They can be sawn, filed, bored or nailed. Thermolite Ytong (autoclaved lime lightweight concrete) and Siporex (autoclaved lightweight concrete) are among some of the brand names.

If the exposed concrete is not fully hardened, the outer layer can be removed by washing and brushing. As with exposed aggregate concrete, the appearance of the surface is determined by the aggregate used. Tests indicate that the type and colour of the aggregate gravel should be kept constant.

Surface-setting retardants, applied to the shuttering, permit larger areas of insitu concrete to be finished as exposed aggregate concrete (see page 61).

Sand blasting of the insitu concrete surface produces a texture similar to that of concrete with a fine aggregate and sand mix. Because the sand blasting removes some of the surface from the concrete, the initial concrete cover to the reinforcement must be thicker. Moderate stone dressing allows concrete to be treated similarly to limestone, but here the initial cover must be much greater to allow for this. For this reason, stone dressing methods are not satisfactory as a means of saving an unsuccessful exposed concrete surface.

Rough surfaces soil more quickly than smooth surfaces. The soiling on the latter is nevertheless noticeable earlier, and they are therefore made water-repellent. The fresh concrete is saturated with a water-proofing agent, and a final coat of silicone is applied (see page 20 above).

Building with large **precast concrete components** in big construction works offer some attractive advantages: small dimensional tolerances, uniform concrete quality and rapid constructional progress.

These panels are mostly sandwich panels manufactured with an integral layer of insulation material. For precast concrete components, lightweight concrete is also used.

Grey concrete hand consolidated B300

Aggregates:	Rhein gravel	
	0— 3 mm	= 25.5%
	3— 7 mm	= 22.5%
	7—30 mm	= 52.0%
Granular additive:	Lime stone dust	
	0—0.2 mm	= 0.5%
	total aggregate weight	
Cement:	PC375	= 310 kg/m³
Concrete additive:	—	
Water cement ratio:	$\frac{W}{C}$	= 0.56
Slump dimension:	S	= 40 cm
Consolidated:	hand consolidated with a rod (steel sheet fixed to a batten)	

Grey concrete B300

Aggregates:	Rhein gravel	
	0— 3 mm	= 30.0%
	3— 7 mm	= 21.0%
	7—15 mm	= 24.5%
	15—30 mm	= 24.5%
Granular additive:	Quartz sand	
	0—0.2 mm	= 4% of total aggregate weight
Cement:	PC275	= 300 kg/m³
Concrete additive:	DM	
Water cement ratio:	$\frac{W}{C}$	= unknown
Slump dimension:	S	= 40 cm
Consolidation:	Needle vibrator with simultaneous shuttering knocks	

Grey concrete B450

Aggregates:	Rhein gravel	
	0— 3 mm	= 30%
	3— 7 mm	= 18%
	7—15 mm	= 28%
	15—30 mm	= 24%
Granular additive:	—	
Cement:	PC275	= 340 kg/m³
Concrete additive:	BV	
Water cement ratio:	$\frac{W}{C}$	= 0.51
Slump dimension:	S	= 34 cm
Consolidation:	needle vibrator	

White concrete B450

Aggregates:	Rhein gravel	
	0— 3 mm	= 30.0%
	3— 7 mm	= 21.0%
	7—15 mm	= 24.5%
	15—30 mm	= 24.0%
Granular additive:	fine white quartz sand	
	0—0.2 mm	= 3% of total aggregate weight
Cement:	PC275 (Dyckerhoff-White)	
Concrete additive:	BV	= 340 kg/m³
Water cement ratio:	$\frac{W}{C}$	= 0.48
Slump dimension:	S	= 32 cm
Consolidation:	needle vibrator with simultaneous shuttering knocks	

Table 9. Exposed concrete mixes tested in practice (from Bacher/Heinle: *Construction in Exposed Concrete* – Julius Hoffmann Verlag, Stuttgart)

Note: For further whitening of the concrete a white pigment (titanium dioxide) can be added to the white cement (2% of the total cement weight).

Mortar bedded panels

The structural wall surface dimensions, including openings and piers should be related to the actual size of the panel, and careful consideration must also be given to the position of the joints.

Almost all mortar bedded panels used in facade construction are highly water repellent and **diffusion of moisture vapour** can only take place through the joints. For this reason the joint width must be related to the panel size and the anticipated moisture transmission. If there is a vapour barrier on the inside of the wall, the joints may be proportionally less wide.

Small sectional coverings have a larger total joint area and generally provide better conditions for moisture diffusion. Rule of thumb cannot be applied in these circumstances, and in cases of doubt the anticipated moisture loading and its dispersal should be calculated by a physicist (see page 53).

Dark coloured panels absorb more heat more readily than lighter coloured panels (see page 11) and this can cause damage due to heat expansion. In hot weather they can increase the temperature of the warm air currents which flow over the facade and enter the rooms through open windows.

Panels are normally bedded in cement mortar and they should not be greater than one storey high, and should be separated by a bearing corbel or wall projection. Wall areas should be divided every 3-6 metres horizontally by an expansion joint. Expansion joints formed in the base construction must not be covered over, but should be carried right through the mortar bed and the surface covering.†

Glass and ceramic mosaic

Normal sizes 20/20/4 mm, special sizes (up to 20/90 and 40/40 mm) to order. Delivered loose or stuck onto backing paper.

Ceramic panels

The following ceramic panels are
Ceramic split clinker slabs (also coloured and glazed), swallow tail nibs on the rear face. Sizes: 24.5/12 cm, 24/7.1 cm, 24/5.2 cm 13-20 mm thick.†

Fused clinker (usually clinker coloured), sizes similar to wall clinker blocks and split clinker flags 16/20 mm thick.†

Faience panels may be glazed or unglazed. Whether as small strips or medium sized mosaic, they are manufactured with paper stuck to the face side of the panel and are bedded in mortar in this way. When they are set the paper is removed.

Natural stone slips can be delivered in various stones and sizes.

Expansion and movement joints

Joints between large-surface building components must be sealed with a mastic, permanently resilient sealing material. Jointing materials must be durable and sufficiently adhesive, whilst being able to withstand the deformation necessary to take up the movements of the building components, including thermal expansion, and creep and shrinkage of concrete.

Joint edges of concrete components should have a firm, dense, surface. Bonding surfaces should be dry and clean in order to ensure adhesion and setting of the mastic. Form-stripping agents, if used, should be previously tested to ascertain whether washing-out will be necessary to avoid loss of adhesion. This also applies where other materials are used.

	up to 2	over 2-4	over 4-6	over 6-8
Joint width b	15	20	25	30
Depth of joint t	30	40	50	60

Table 10. Minimum dimensions in mm for joints sealed with mastic (from DIN 18540, 'Design')

There are various joint sealing sections made from plastic on the market, these are used for sealing insitu concrete structures and are concreted in.

Glass

Glass bricks

Walls built of glass bricks must be able to move freely at all abutments. Adequate expansion joints should be provided which must not be subsequently rendered over in recesses and openings but be allowed to move freely.

The width of the wall depends on the brick size, reinforcement, bonding, and wind load, as does the maximum surface area (6-24 m²). Reference should be made to manufacturers' tables.

Similar structural considerations apply to concrete glass surfaces, which for better thermal insulation can be installed with two layers of glass. Generally concreting of the surface components is done before they are assembled.

Steel reinforcement should only be used where sufficient concrete cover to the steel ensures that rusting will not occur.

Profilit

For large glass surfaces cast glass with a 'U' section is available (widths 22, 25, 32 mm; depths 4.1 and 6.0 cm; glass thickness 6-7 mm respectively; largest length 7 m). Sheet glass can also be obtained with a spot-welded wire mesh inserted, and may be installed in one or two layers. How large a Profilit wall should be depends upon the type of glass used and the height above the ground. Joints are sealed with mastic or PVC sections. The abutments should be treated in the same wall as for glass bricks.

Cellular glass

Cellular glass components consist of 2 panes of cast glass (rough cast, ornamental glass, wired glass) which are separated at a distance of 12 mm by glass cross ribs, spaced at about 6-10 mm from each other. The sheet sizes are obtainable up to 4.5 m high and 90 cm wide. Sealing at abutments is achieved by using a preformed mastic tape with an additional sealing mastic on the outside (see page 68).

Suspended glazing

For an approximate pane size of 4-5 m high it is best for the glass to be suspended. The glass is not usually pre-tensioned and is fixed to an accurately adjustable steel frame construction. A 1 cm gap is left open at the bottom of the recess. Stiffening is by glass stabilising channels or, for greater heights, a combined glass/metal mullion. Pane widths should not be greater than 300 cm. Pane heights generally 450 up to 800 cm (present maximum 11 m). Pane thickness 12-22 mm.

Pre-tensioned glass

Single pane safety glass is more shatter-proof than ordinary glass. In breaking it does not produce dangerous splinters, and is therefore more suitable for use in facades than ordinary glass. It cannot, however, be cut or worked afterwards. For this reason the pane sizes and opening dimensions must be established when ordering the glass. For non-standard requirements, details of the actual pane sizes should be submitted.

For fixing into clamp framing, 'U' sections, or brickwork joints, or for assembly with metal mountings, an interface layer must be placed between the glass and the abutting material, eg, 1-1.5 mm of Presspan. In bored holes corresponding bushes should be inserted.

The stability of all glass installations is achieved by the metal mountings. Putty or similar material is not necessary. If it is to be a watertight construction, only permanently resilient mastics should be used for sealing.

Pre-tensioned glass is assembled in the usual fashion and is not suspended. The present maximum pane sizes may be used without further precautions. Opening lights, doors and switchgear etc, can be attached to constructions which should not be subjected to loads. For these purposes there are simplified methods of assembly generally in use with steel section clamping devices for which small edge notches are required.

In some cases sheets of pre-tensioned glass break for no apparent reason (this is known as spontaneous fracture). Present knowledge suggests the probable cause to be microscopic particles of nickel sulphide, which expand in the course of time and shatter the glass. Manufacturers cannot ensure a nickel sulphide free glass, and the panes should be subjected to a heat test in which faulty glass will shatter. (In these tests the glass is heated for three hours at a temperature of 240°C).

If **two-pane safety glass** is used in external walls, the continuous glued joint around the edges of the glass must be protected against weathering.

The glass panes must be installed so as to avoid all tensions. Clear glass is subject to considerable heat absorption.

Sun protection glass

Thermolux is a laminated glass with a bonded-in layer of glass fibre (generally white). It produces a soft, diffused light, and reduces heat radiation.

Thermal insulation glasses, such as Contracalor, Katacalor, or Parsol, transmit visible light clearly but with a reduction in intensity and with a slight tint. They mainly act by absorbing the ultra-violet light from the sun more effectively than clear or coloured glass which do not possess this quality. As this glass warms up, it can act as a secondary heating surface. For this reason it is often installed in front of the facade to allow the air to flow right round it.

Thermex is a two-pane laminated glass with a light sensitive plastic layer in between. As this glass becomes warm, the plastic layer turns to a milky white, thus reducing radiation transmission. When mounted externally in front of the facade this reaction of the plastic layer takes place more quickly.

Reflective glasses such as Cudo-Gold, Cudo-Aurisin or Cudo-Grey are laminates in which the external surface has on its inside face an extremely thin layer of gold, which increases the reflective quality of the glass and reduces the visible light and heat radiation.

Many tests have been carried out in the field of sun protection glazing and expert advice should be obtained in cases of doubt.

Rear ventilated cladding

Even though a wall cladding plays an important part in determining the *appearance* of a building, its main role is to provide a protective surface. It improves wind and weather protection as well as resistance against physical and chemical attack.

When such a skin is rear ventilated, **damp concentration** can be avoided. These can otherwise reduce the thermal insulation of the wall considerably, and can lead to building damage. Timber shingles are among the oldest of the rear ventilated cladding, forming a protective shell which is easily repaired or replaced.

Joints between sections of a cladding can remain open provided the substructure and its external layer of thermal insulation remain watertight, and driving rain cannot penetrate at the junctions of doors and windows. Expansion joints of the supporting structure must also extend through the cladding. At no point should the cladding be rigidly bridged (see page 22). Where cladding components overlap each other, the direction of laying should oppose that of the prevailing wind. The assembly of individual components should commence on the sheltered side and should run from bottom to top.

Timber, timber protection and surface treatment of timber

For centuries timber has proved itself an excellent elevational material, as proved by the timber houses in Scandinavia, the Black Forest and elsewhere, numerous home grown and foreign timbers are suitable (see Table 12). Failures can, as a rule, be traced back to faulty construction or workmanship. It is mainly a question of fungal attack which results from a high moisture content and which causes decay; insect attack (capricorn beetle, *Anobium punctatum*) does not appear very often in facade timbers.

Precautions taken for timber protection

1. **Construction precautions,** which in particular should aim to minimise moisture concentration in the timber (a pre-requisite for the onset of fungal attack).

With appropriate construction and treatment, even non-durable kinds of timber, may be used unprotected on normally stressed facades and these will function satisfactorily for many years. The more protection timber gets from overhanging roofs, the wider the choice of suitable timber and method of construction. As a general guide to precautions to be taken during construction the following may be of use (see also DIN 68800 'Timber Protection in Building Construction', sheet 2, 'Preventive Structural Precautions') Water collection areas should be avoided at corners, grooves and abutments. With horizontal cladding a groove must always be formed in the lower edge; vertical cladding should always be avoided on the main prevailing weather side of the building. The space between timber cladding and abutments should be such that no water concentration occurs, and edges and rebates have sufficient fall to carry the water away to the outside (see pages 76-85).

Shingles may be split or sawn. Timbers which are especially suitable are fir trees, eg, larch and red cedar (see example on pages 86-87). Timber cladding should terminate at least 30 cm above ground level. The major considerations are adequate cross section and rear ventilation.

2. Choice of **naturally durable timbers** and suitable treatments, (eg, waterproof adhesives, functionally durable sealing materials).

3. **Application of chemical timber protection treatments.** Only officially recognised and tested preparations should be used, lists of which are issued by several sources. Timber protection should also take account of the back of cladding materials and the base construction. By using pigmented preparations (protective varnishes and the like), a toned surface can be achieved during maintenance of the timber structure.

Outer surface treatments of timber facades are required in order to avoid the greying effect which takes place with all timbers when they are exposed to the weathering influences of sun and rain. The most important systems are:

Film forming paints, which restrict moisture movement and thus reduce expansion and contraction of the timber. At the same time, however, they have a delaying effect on the drying out process in timber components which have become damp. In the course of time the paint film splits, exposing the underlying timber. The painted surfaces must be renewed, in the case of clear varnished surfaces at regular intervals of 1-3 years, and with opaque varnishes every 3-7 years. It is worth recommending the use of timber protecting primers.

Non-film forming paints (wrongly termed 'open pored') do not restrict moisture movement or expansion and contraction of the timber and they permit timber components which are damp to dry out properly. In the course of time they will fade, and must be given regular treatment with the appropriate preservative. With the use of transparent and pigmented varnishes the timber structure is preserved. With dispersion paints a result will be achieved similar to that of opaque varnish. Coats will have to be renewed more regularly than with opaque varnishes – every 2-4 years – but the task is straight forward and causes no problems.

Shingles

Spruce and larch shingles should be hand-split and immersed in a suitable preservation for a four-week period before use to

Hardwoods (deciduous)

Type of timber	origin	colour	average gross density with 15% moisture content	durability	remarks	painting directions
Hardwoods (deciduous)						
Afrormosia (Kokrodua)	Ghana, Zaire, Cameroons	brown	0.75	a	strong iron corrosion and staining	constituent materials delay drying
Agba (Tola branca)	Angola, Zaire, Nigeria, Ghana	yellow/pink/brown	0.5	b	high resin content	moderately difficult due to resin
Doussie (Afzelia)	Tropical West Africa	dark brown	0.8	a	strong iron corrosion and staining	difficult due to constituent material
Oak	Europe, America	brown/yellow	0.7	b-c	strong iron staining	relatively simple
Iroko (Kambala)	Tropical East and West Africa	gold/brown	0.7	a	strong iron corrosion and staining	constituent materials delay drying
Mansonia	West Africa, Cameroons up to the Elephant Leg Coasts	olive/violet/brown	0.65	a	saw dust is dangerous to health	constituent materials delay drying
Teak	Java, Madoera, Siam, Burma, Indo-China, Further India	light gold/brown to dark brown	0.7	a	very good bearing capacity	difficult due to constituent materials
Sipo-Mahogany	Tropical West Africa	red/brown	0.65	b	—	moderately difficult due to constituent materials
Softwoods (coniferous)						
Spruce (Pica excelsa)	Middle/NE Europe, Western Siberia	yellowish white	0.45	d		
Scots pine (Pinus sylvestris)	Middle/NE Europe, Siberia	dark yellow/red brown	0.5	c-d		
Larch (Larix Europa)	Middle/NE Europe, NE Asia, Japan, British Columbia, Montana, Canada, North East USA	stripes red/brown	0.65	c		
Pitchpine	East and South USA, Central America	orange/brown	0.7	c	trademarks for various kinds of pine	relatively difficult due to constituent materials
Redwood	California, Oregon	yellow/brown to red/brown	0.35	b		
Fir (Abies)	Central and Southern Europe	reddish/yellow	0.45	d		
Oregon pine (Douglas Fir)	West Coast of North America	yellowish/brown to red/brown	0.55	c	very resinous, iron staining	
Red cedar	West side of North America from South Alaska to North California	brown (when dry)	0.35	b	iron corrosion and staining	

Table 11. Tests for durability have extended over many years in Britain, in which the timber in constant contact with the moist earth remained healthy

a more than 25 years
b 15 to 25 years
c 10 to 15 years
d 5 to 10 years

guard against decay. Cedar shingles imported from Canada and the USA are considerably more durable and no more expensive. The timber of the 'Western Red Cedar' (*Thuja plicta*) is very resistant to decaying fungi by virtue of its natural composition.

It is important to differentiate between 'shingles,' which are sawn, and 'shakes' which are split. Shingles are frequently used which are produced by sawing diagonally across the crude log; this produces two tapering shingles, the split side being used face upwards. Standard lengths are 40 cm. A lattice pattern of battens, on vertical surfaces at 19 cm centres, provides a two-layer and frequently a three-layer shingle covering with the batten centres at 13 cm.

The Material Testing Establishment of the University of Stuttgart determined after a fire test in 1969, that a three-layer shingle roof, in terms of DIN 4102 ('Fire Resistance of Building Components') could be considered as a 'solid roofing'.†

Slates and asbestos cement shingles

Facades can be clad with natural slates, (see pages 88 and 89). Frequently today small sized asbestos cement sheets are used, (see pages 90 and 91), which can also be produced with attrative surfaces in various colours (thickness 3.2 and 4.0 mm).

Natural slates are usually nailed to continuous boarding (with non-ferrous nails of course); for larger asbestos cement sheets a lattice of battens is adequate.

Asbestos cement sheets

Flat asbestos cement sheets in large sizes are laid without overlaps, the usual method of fixing is to screw through to the base construction. However, there are now sheets available with invisible lugs on the back for securing to brackets.

For sealing the joints and the corners, window openings, etc, of the building, purpose-made components have been developed by manufacturers.

Glass sheets

Of all building materials, glass is the easiest to clean because of its sealed polished surface. Rear ventilated sheets can be fixed vertically or horizontally with a continuous glazing bead or with individual clips. Besides cladding the external window sill aprons in opaque or coloured glass sheets, glass also offers the possibility of enclosing the whole building in a continuous glass 'screen', as shown on page 101; which can also provide considerable sound protection.

In the building shown on page 108, the 12 mm glass panes of the curtain wall provide a sound insulation improvement of 10 dB, and the energy costs were reduced by 10 per cent (see also page 23).

Glass sheets must be fixed so that no tensions are transmitted through the sheets.

Natural stone slabs

So as to be suitable for external wall cladding, natural stone must possess a specific durability and weather resistance. The colour of the sawn, split or polished stones is an inadequate

criterion since the atmosphere in large cities presents a major problem. The slabs are also very heavy. A granite slab of 1 sq m area and 4 cm thick weighs 110 kp, and a travertine marble slab of the same size and thickness 100 kp. These loads have to be considered, not only in erecting the slabs but also in fixing them to the building. They must also be included in the dead loading of the building.

The **minimum possible thickness** is related to the slab size, the durability to the proven breaking load of the slab at the point of anchorage and to the external loads such as wind and suction loads.

The normal slab size should not exceed 1 s qm when a thickness of 3 cm for harder stones is sufficient; for softer stones the thickness should be 4-5 cm.†

The laying-in of facade slabs with dabs or strips of mortar is not permissible. A full bed of mortar, together with sheradized anchors, is essential in the ground storey. In upper storeys, rear ventilated slabs are permitted only when fixed with stainless steel cramps and bearers; every slab must be fixed so that it is entirely self-supporting. It should rest on two bearers and be prevented from overturning by two hook cramps.

Joints can be filled with mortar or mastic and, as previously mentioned, may be left open in certain conditions. At every floor level expansion joints must be provided of at least 1 cm wide, as well as vertical expansion joints about 3-6 m apart.† All distance pieces, cramps, mortar, etc, must be kept out of expansion joints so that transmission of any load is avoided. **Expansion joints** should be sealed finally with mastic.

Artificial stone and ceramic slabs

Slabs can be made from artificial stone or with exposed aggregates similar to natural stone slabs, as, too, can concrete slabs with ceramic tiles bonded to the visible surface. What has been previously said in the section 'Natural stone slabs' concerning fixing and formation of joints is also applicable here.

Where such slabs are used as **permanent shuttering** and are concreted in, it is necessary to determine the means for moisture diffusion from the interior to the external air, with thought given to wall construction, vapour barriers, provision of small condensation channels for removal of water etc.

The brick industry produces large slabs with exposed surfaces of split bricks which can either be mounted as rear ventilated claddings or bonded to hollow clay bricks which provide continuous **vertical ventilation** cavities, permitting rain and condensation moisture to be carried away.

Cast light metal

Cast aluminium is lightweight, rigid and weather resistant. It can be cast in large, thin sheets. For surfaces of 1 m² the thickness is approximately 6 mm, and for 3 m² approximately 10 mm, which corresponds to about 27 kg/m². The sheets are assembled using hooks or some other form of attachment which are either cast into the sheet or welded on.

The simplest and therefore the most economical form of casting is the **oven-pouring process,** in which the alloy is poured into flat, open moulds filled with sand. The exposed surface hardens in the atmosphere. The structure of the metal can be affected by the alloying as well as by the skill of the craftsmen in the casting. Sheets are of sizes up to 3.5 by 2.0 m. A technically convenient size of casting is about 2.0 by 1.0 m.

If texturing of the exposed surface is desired (from fine grained surfacing to strong relief) casting into enclosed sand moulds is necessary. For this, sheet sizes generally go up to 1.8 by 1.5 m. By a process developed in Japan, three-dimensional facade elements can be poured and these can be of 6-8 mm thickness, up to 4 m high and 1.8 m wide.† The examples on pages 112 and 113 demonstrate how many and varied are the possibilities. Moreover the surface can take any structure or colour that is wanted, and it can be anodised, covered with plastic paint or enamelled.

Sheet metals

These may be divided into three groups:

Flat sheets. The metal sheets are simply lapped at the edges, and have no inherent stiffness. For this reason reflective sheets (eg refined steel), are often mounted on panels or have some other form of stiffening. Dull sheet metals such as lead, copper, or Cor-Ten do not need this.

Cassettes are deep drawn or pressed sheets and because of their form are inherently stiff. Most of the firms concerned offer various cassette types. For larger buildings special forms are used almost exclusively. It is particularly important that the elements are related to the planning grid, sill and storey dimensions of the building. A large number of units justifies the manufacture of special tools. Smaller elements are cheaper to produce but more expensive to instal. At the design stage, thought should be given to pollution (dust, rainwater run-off), and subsequent cleaning. It should also be remembered that, because of the light reflection, a polished metal produces a stronger expression of plastic forms than a matt surface.

Profile strips. The advantage of profile strips lies in the fact that they can be delivered in long lengths and are easily assembled, eg, on fixing clips which correspond to the profile section. The section can also take up thermal expansion movement which, for large surfaces, can be considerable. Related in form are slender profile sections which are clipped on individually, and extruded sections.

The following metals are used:

Steel can be protected against rust by galvanising, enamelling or covering with plastic. It is also essential that internal parts, cut edges, bored holes, etc, are protected against corrosion. With the use of refined steels this trouble is avoided (cost permitting).

Weathering steel. Since 1933 the United States Steel Corporation has produced a highly resistant weathering steel under the brand name of Cor-Ten (the name being formed from *cor*rosion resistant and *ten*sile strength). In 1964 Saarinen used this steel in unprotected situations in the Administration Building of the Deere Corporation in Moline, Illinois. This steel is also produced in Germany by the Thyssen Niederheim Co.

Cor-Ten is a low alloy steel which on exposure to the air forms a brown/violet patina-like layer that protects against rust and prevents further corrosion of the metal beneath.

At the start of the corrosion process rain washes off rust particles, which leads to staining of underlying parts of the building. Construction precautions for controlling the sediment from rain water should be given very careful consideration at the design stage.

From the point of view of its mechanical properties, Cor-Ten corresponds to Building Steel 52-3; also related to it is Patinex of the Building Steel 37-2. Weather resistant steels are 13-18% dearer, but because painting costs can be excluded, the total building costs are not higher than those for common building steel.

Weather resistant steels are, generally speaking, preferred for steel building construction, pipe bridges, and bridge construction, storage silos, and for pipeline construction.

Cor-Ten and Patinex have stood the test well in heavily polluted atmospheres. In areas where industrial gas is heavily concentrated, weather resistant steels without paint protection are not recommended; nor are they on sea coasts, under water, or in the ground, where persistent dampness is to be expected.

Aluminium is lighter than other metals (specific weights: copper 8.9, steel 7.8, aluminium 2.7 kp/dm³). Its thermal expansion co-efficient is about twice that of the steel/concrete relationship. Thermal movement of aluminium cladding must be absorbed by suitable forms of construction such as folds or sliding seams or by non-rigid fastenings.

Copper, steel and bronze should not be in contact with unprotected aluminium, and base construction must be rust-proofed to avoid damage from corrosion. Galvanised, chrome, or cadmium steels, stainless steels and zinc do not attack aluminium. Concrete or mortar which is not completely cured (green) should be covered with a coat of bitumastic paint, building paper, or plastic sheet (fully cured concrete is not harmful). The same goes for fire retardant impregnators and timber protection treatments; oil or oil types on a phosphate base are also harmless.

Untreated aluminium forms an oxide film on its surface which, depending on the degree of pollution, becomes medium or dark grey. The most common treatment for aluminium is anodising, in which an artificial thin oxide film is formed on the surface, which keeps its metallic appearance, either in natural tone or transparent colours.

By enamelling, stove enamelling or plastic sheathing, almost any surface colour can be produced, but all these treatments are factory produced.

Copper oxidises quickly to a deep brown or almost black tone. On old copper roofs a green patina used to form, but in the cleaner city atmospheres of today this no longer happens. When rain water runs down from copper surfaces, limestone and concrete are stained green.

Lead sheeting is weather resistant, malleable and suitable for facade cladding (see page 105).

Plastic

For facade cladding rigid PVC (polyvinyl chloride), GRP (glass reinforced unsaturated polyester), PMMA 'Perspex' (Polymethylmethacrylate) and others are used for folded plate, sheet pile and hollow sections and for cassettes.

Plastics have a low relative weight, a good colour range, and can be easily formed by extrusion, vacuum moulding, or pressing.

Given suitable quality, large expanses of plastic can withstand both distortion and weathering.

For facades plastics of low flammability are specified. These may be used up to the boundaries of high rise dwellings, but only on walls without openings.

Plastics have a high thermal expansion co-efficient (in 70° temperature variation the length increase is per metre for PVC 5.6 mm, PMMA 4.9 mm, GRP 1.8 mm, aluminium 1.5 mm, concrete 0.7 mm). For this reason allowance must be made for adequate tolerances. Vertical, continuous sheet pile sections and horizontal hollow sections must have at least one expansion joint per storey; all fastenings must be capable of movement (slotted holes etc).

Cassettes are produced by a deep drawn process, with sizes determined by that of the building. By virtue of their form, they are able to absorb thermal expansion movement without any marked effect. Sizes available are generally in the region of 1.25/3.00 m.

Base constructions for rear ventilated cladding

The base construction should not interrupt the rear ventilation; conversely, the air space should not be too large (the 'Principles concerning the Use of Combustible Materials in Building Construction' require a rear ventilation cavity of 4 cm maximum so that, with a combustible building material, the fire does not spread behind the cladding).† The simplest form of base construction is of battens and counter battens.

Combustible materials are permitted up to a height of two storeys. They are also permitted in higher walls, especially in surfaces where there are no windows.

When using base constructions of **metal,** special attention must be given to the prevention of corrosion (see also page 28).

For many wall claddings, special base constructions are available which make installation simpler. On page 116 an example is shown of sheets **without a base construction** screwed directly into plugs set in the wall.

With insitu concrete walls, channels, anchors, battens, and similar fixing aids should be placed into the formwork before the concrete is poured.

Curtain walls

Framed structures make it possible for the external wall to relinquish its traditional load bearing task and function only as a space enclosure. Lightweight, high-value insulation materials protected between waterproof layers, make it possible to design light curtain walls, in which the windows and apron panels lie in the same plane, in contrast to rear ventilated cladding where windows are fixed into the carcass construction.

With light curtain walls (under 300 kp/m²) DIN 4108 'Thermal Insulation in Building Construction' lays down that the minimum thermal transmission resistance must be increased in relation to the lightness of the wall as an adjustment for the low heat storage capacity (see also page 10).†

Mullion construction

Mullions generally run vertically in front of the floor slabs. The window and apron panels are assembled individually or as storey height units. The fewer intermediate mullions that are necessary, the larger the units become, and the problems of joint sealing are concentrated in fewer places facilitating speed of installation. Whilst formerly mullions dictated the appearance of the facade, there are numerous recent examples in which window panels completely dominate the main vertical mullions (see pages 130, 131, 137).

Framed construction

Windows and window panels are formed as storey height units, preformed and without mullions. They are joined directly to each other and fixed to the building structure. The facade members are in one plane or are interrupted by projecting walls and/or infil panels (eg, page 133).

For mullion and framed construction the sections are generally of drawn aluminium or clad in stainless steel.

Timber construction has also been developed (eg, page 133). The window panels are generally damp proofed sandwich panels with exposed surfaces of glass, asbestos cement, metal sheets, plastic etc.

Panel construction

This section refers to curtain walls in which elements of at least storey height are connected directly with each other and are mounted in front of the main building structure (see page 140). These developments have come about as more labour is withdrawn from the building site and transferred to the factory.

The panels are mainly constructed in panel form, the window being formed with rounded corners, similar to car body construction and installed without mitred abutments.

In England facade elements of plastic have been developed, with steel frames inserted. They are so light in weight that up to six elements (three storeys high, two bays wide) were assembled in the factory, transported to the site and erected as one arge unit.

Heavy panels

Storey height units of precast concrete, with insulation and windows provided, are delivered to the site and mounted as a curtain wall (see page 151). They therefore do not take floor loads, and for this reason units have now been developed which extend over several storeys (see page 50).

Exposed frames

At one time with curtain walls, the columns were placed behind the facade, but more recent developments, by Skidmore, Owings and Merill, have reversed this procedure by placing concrete load bearing frames in front of the facade. These components are precast and act as pin-jointed columns transmitting only horizontal loads.

This form of construction is not suitable for high-rise blocks of dwellings. All the same, designs have been developed for exceptionally high buildings – including a steel frame with large diagonal bracing standing in front of the facade – which are claimed as the most economical method to date (eg, John Hancock Centre Chicago, 337 m high).

Structural calculations and costings for these types of structures are only really possible with the aid of computers.

Relevant DIN sheets

From the large number of DIN sheets of German standards, the following have been selected as the most important for external wall construction. The latest edition should be taken as the most authoritative.

DIN sheets can be obtained in Germany from: Beuth-Vertrieb, 1 Berlin 30, Berggrafenstrasse 4-7; 5 Köln 1, Friesenplatz 16; 6 Frankfurt-am-Main 1, Gutleutestrasse 163.

In Britain DIN sheets can be obtained from British Standards Institution, 101 Pentonville Road, London N1 9ND; and in the USA from

DIN	Edition	
4102	2/1970	Fire resistance of building materials
4100	8/1969	Thermal protection in building construction
4109	9/1962	Noise protection in building construction
18005	5/1971	Sheet 1 standard: Noise protection in urban construction
5034	12/1969	Internal space illumination by daylight
18050	9/1955	Window openings for domestic construction: Carcassing—guide dimensions
1053	11/1962	Brickwork: Calculation and construction
18332	12/1958	Contract procedure for building works – Part C: General provisions for natural stonework
183350	12/1958	Contract procedure for building works – Part C: General provisions for rendering and stucco work
18333	12/1958	Contract procedure for building works – Part C: General provisions for concrete block construction
18330	12/1958	Contract procedure for building works – Part C: General provisions for brickwork
105	7/1969	Bricks: Solid and perforated bricks
106	4/1969	Calcium silicate bricks: Solid, perforated, and hollow block bricks
4166	2/1959	Wall slabs of autoclaved foamed and aerated concrete
274	3/1970	Sheet 1 Design: Corrugated asbestos
18515	7/1970	Facade cladding in natural stone, concrete blocks and ceramic materials Specifications for the construction process
18155	1/1962	Ceramic wall and floor tiles
18166	7/1965	Split ceramic slabs
1249	8/1952	Sheet glass: Thickness and types, testing and dimensions
4242	1/1967	Glass brick walls: Construction and dimemensions
18361	12/1958	Contract procedure for building works – Part C: General provisions for glazing work
1050	6/1968	Steel in building construction
4113	2/1958	Aluminium in building construction: Specification for calculation and construction of aluminium building components
68121	12/1968	Timber window sections: Side, top hung and pivot windows
18055	4/1971	Sheet 2 Design: Joint tightness and driving rain protection: Requirements and testing
18540	4/1971	Sheet 1 Design: Waterproofing of external wall joints between insitu concrete and reinforced concrete precast components with sealing joint dimensions: Construction formation of joints
52175	6/1954	Timber protection: Principles, suggestions
	4/1971	Design for timber protection: Suggestions, principles
68800	9/1956	Timber protection in building construction

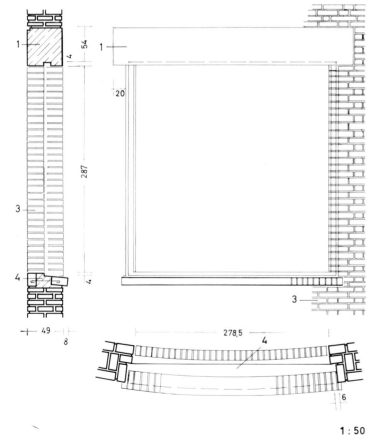

Church of St Boniface, Wetzlar, Germany
Architects: Dr Ing Rudolf Schwarz and Maria Schwarz, Frankfurt am Main

Traditional bonded construction in multi-coloured bricks. The building was later treated for efflorescence on the brickwork. Concrete window sills with steel ties.

1 : 50

1 Exposed concrete lintel 49/50 cm
2 Concrete soffit
3 Fair faced brickwork, 49 cm, smooth jointed
4 Concreted rebate with steel rotors for roller blinds

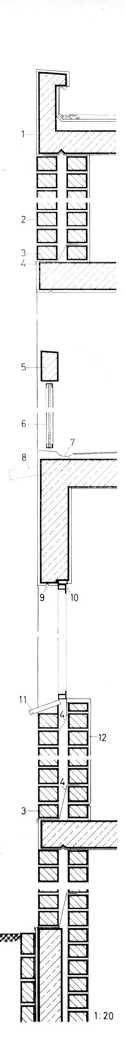

Split level block of flats in Sydney, Australia
Architects: Harry Seidler & Associates, Sydney

Cavity brickwork. For the ventilation of the cavity every fourth
vertical joint is left open in the lowest bed course.

1 Dark grey exposed aggregate rendering on all concrete
   surfaces
2 Light yellow bricks
3 Every fourth vertical course left open in bed course
4 Zinc cavity flashing
5 Precast exposed concrete balcony apron 17/10 cm
6 Grey sheet glass in steel frames painted dark grey
7 Condensation floor channel
8 Plastic pipe
9 Drip groove
10 Single glazed window in aluminium frame anodised dark
   grey
11 Precast concrete sill
12 Plaster

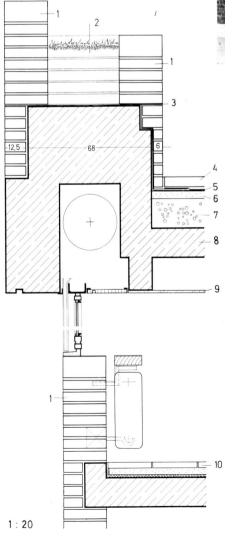

1 : 20

Architect's own house in Cologne
Architect: Oswald M. Ungers, Cologne

The brickwork internally is also exposed facing brickwork.
Single glazed windows, insulating glass, in steel frames.

1 External facing bricks 24 cm, top course as brick on edge capping
2 Flower box
3 1 layer of building paper stuck down
4 Brick paving
5 2 layers of building paper stuck down
6 4 cm cement screed topping
7 Slag screeding laid to falls
8 Reinforced concrete
9 Suspended ceiling
10 Concrete tiles 3 cm

Fair faced brickwork

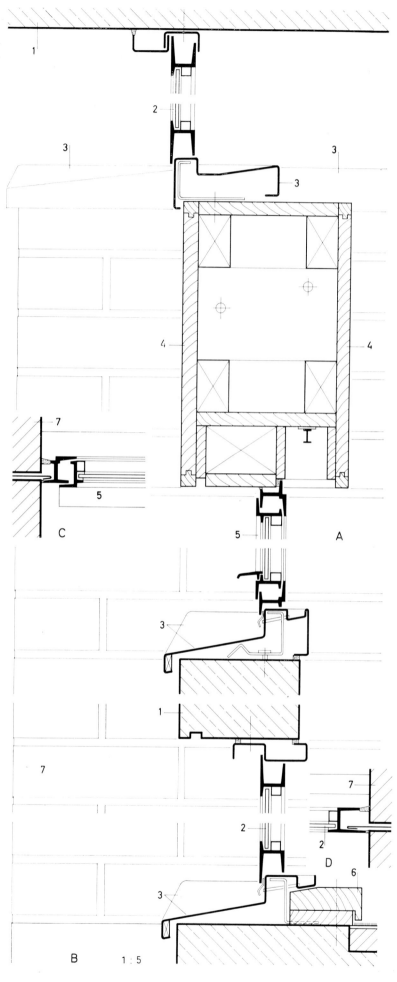

Library of the University of Sussex, England
Architects: Sir Basil Spence, Bonnington & Collins, London

1 Precast concrete eaves unit in faced concrete
2 Fixed glazed steel window
3 Metal flashing
4 Timber spandrel painted white
5 Opening sash
6 Oak sill
7 Red facing brickwork

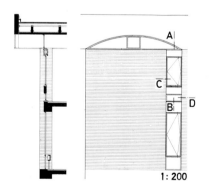

1 : 200

1 : 5

Two skin cavity brickwork. Total thickness 28 cm and 34 cm respectively. The skins are joined with wire ties. They are fixed in the 28 cm thick walls at 90 cm diagonally and 45 cm vertically. In 34 cm walls they are 75 cm and 30 cm distance apart respectively.
Note: In accordance with DIN 1053 these distances should not be exceeded: ie, 75 and 30 cm.

Library of the University of Sussex, England (for details see opposite page)

1 Zinc sheet trim
2 Precast concrete component
3 Silicone painted calcium silicate brickwork
4 Exposed concrete plinth with two layers of building paper under brickwork
5 10 mm air space
6 20 mm plaster board sheets

Housing group in Karlsruhe, Germany
Architects: Dorothea Haupt, Peter Haupt and Ernst Jung, Berlin

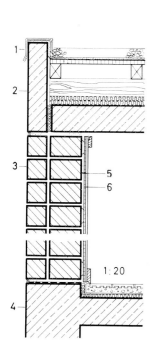

1:20

Fair faced brickwork

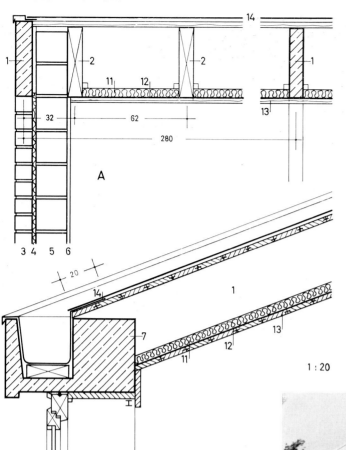

A

B

Architect's own house, Kiel, Germany
Architect: Walter Meyer-Bohe, Kiel

A Patio and load bearing wall
B Non-load bearing wall

1 Precast component
2 Joists 35/8 cm
3 Hand painted Dutch brickwork
4 Polystyrene 16 mm
5 Porous calcium silicate bricks (high porosity)
6 Plaster 15 cm
7 Precast concrete gutter/lintol unit
8 Sipo-mahogany window with insulating glass
9 White calcium silicate bricks, recessed joints, externally white plastic paint (emulsion), internally painted with bitumen
10 Plasterboard 2.5 cm
11 Plasterboard 5 cm
12 Aluminium Kraft paper
13 Oregon pine
14 Eternit shingles

1 : 20

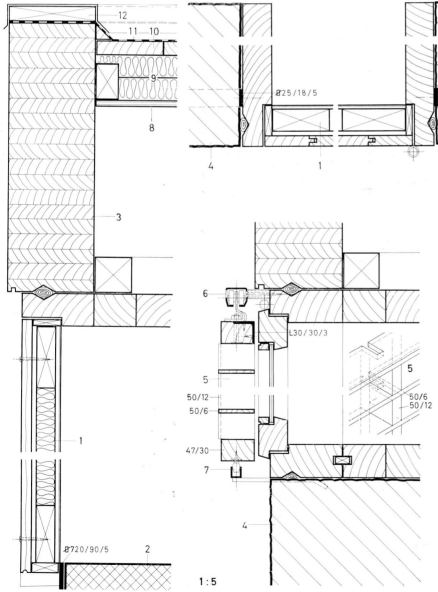

Summer house in St Margarethen, Burgenland, Austria
Architect: Dr Roland Rainer, Vienna

Sealing between walling and frames applied manually.
Frames fixed with flat steel wall cramps 25/5 cm bedded 180 mm in wall.

1 Plywood access door clad internally with spruce, externally with grooved weather boarding 15/65 mm
2 Stone slabs 60 mm
3 Laminated spruce purlins
4 Natural stone walling in St Margarethen sandstone
5 Sliding window shutters
6 Sliding gear channel
7 Guiding wheel in rear channel
8 Plywood sheet cladding 8 mm
9 Glass wool 2/30 mm
10 Timber decking 18 mm
11 Impregnated paper roof covering
12 Acacia wood 120/30 mm covered with a metal trim

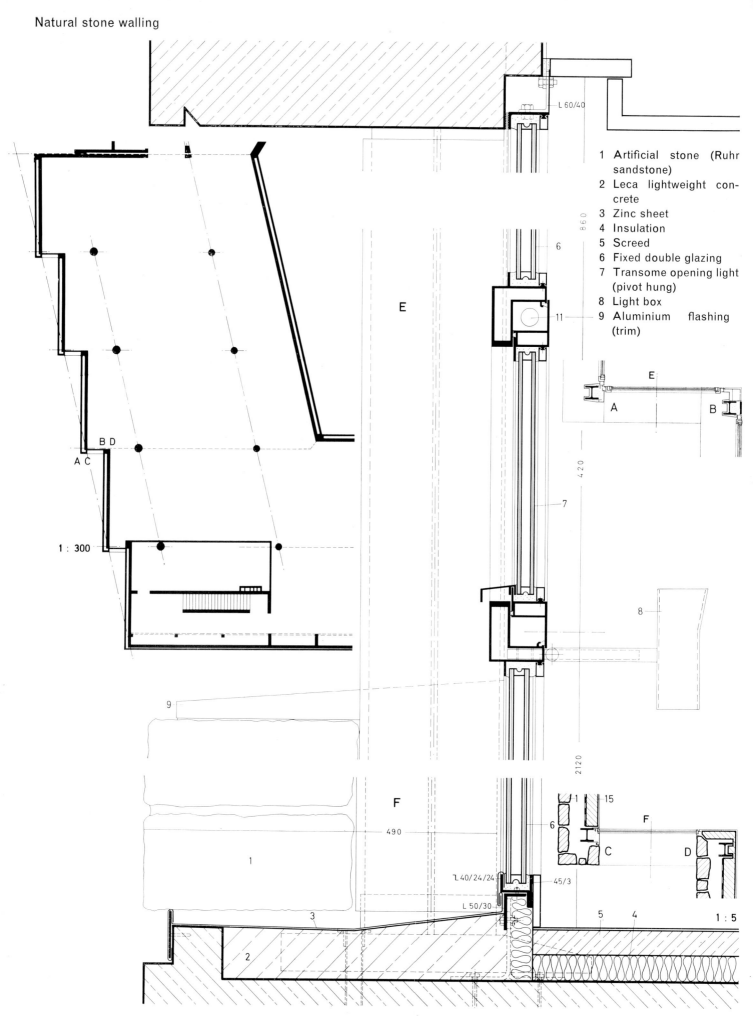

1 Artificial stone (Ruhr sandstone)
2 Leca lightweight concrete
3 Zinc sheet
4 Insulation
5 Screed
6 Fixed double glazing
7 Transome opening light (pivot hung)
8 Light box
9 Aluminium flashing (trim)

L 60/40

860

E

6

11

420

E

A   B

7

8

9

2120

F

1   15

6

490

F

C   D

1

1 : 5

L 40/24/24

45/3

L 50/30

3

2

5   4

1 : 300

B D

A C

History Museum, am Hohen Ufer, Hanover   Architect: Dieter Oesterlen, Hanover

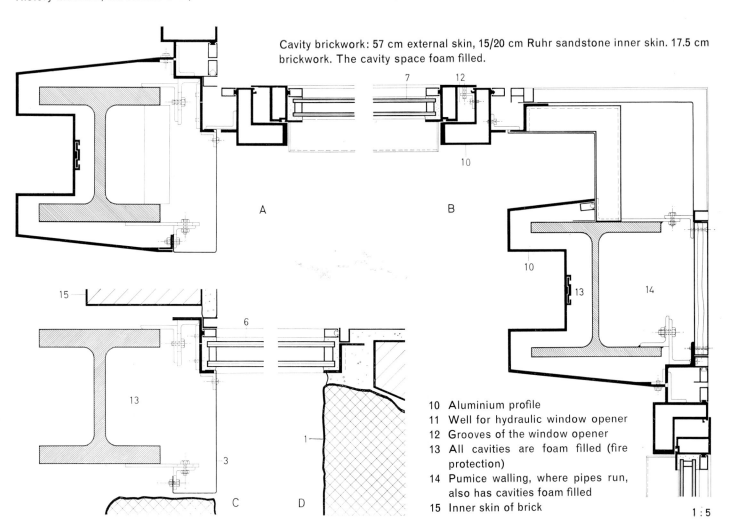

Cavity brickwork: 57 cm external skin, 15/20 cm Ruhr sandstone inner skin. 17.5 cm brickwork. The cavity space foam filled.

A

B

C

D

10 Aluminium profile
11 Well for hydraulic window opener
12 Grooves of the window opener
13 All cavities are foam filled (fire protection)
14 Pumice walling, where pipes run, also has cavities foam filled
15 Inner skin of brick

1 : 5

Mortonhall Crematorium, Edinburgh, Scotland
Architects: Sir Basil Spence, Glover & Ferguson, London and
Edinburgh

The walls are cavity. Externally, concrete block 15 cm thick with white gravel facing. Height of the blocks: 22.5 cm, 45 cm and 60 cm. Width as a rule 75 cm. On corners and slopes they are specially formed. Inner skin of lightweight concrete blocks 10 cm thick with acoustic plaster on the inside. The wall cappings are of zinc.

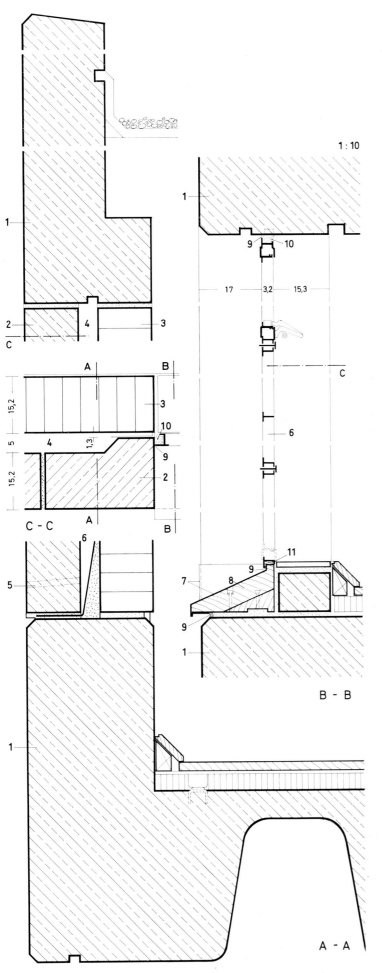

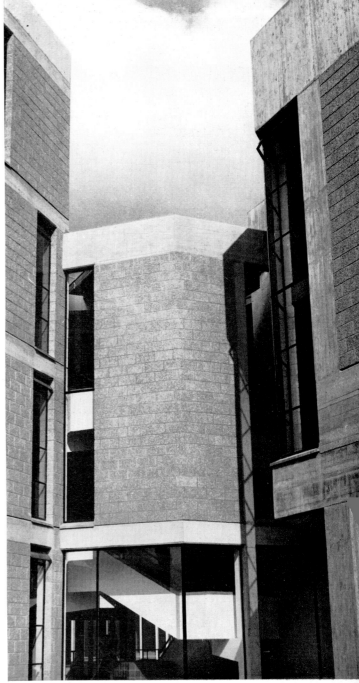

Auditorium of the University of Essex, England
Architects: H. T. Cadbury-Brown & Partners, London

1 Exposed concrete (formwork partly horizontal, partly vertical)
2 Concrete blocks with an applied surface of grey/pink Cornish granite about 45/225 by 15.2 cm thick
3 Lignacite blocks of the same section as 2
4 Air space of 5 cm
5 Ventilation holes every 90 cm in the vertical joints
6 Single glazed aluminium windows
7 Painted zinc window sill covering
8 Impregnated softwood – plugged and screwed
9 Mastic sealing in all joints around window and sill
10 Waterproofed mortar
11 Softwood ground

Lightweight concrete slabs

Architect's house in Drottningholm, Sweden
Architect: Ralph Erskine, Drottningholm

Drottningholm is a small area with brick houses of the eighteenth century on an island 15 km from the centre of Stockholm.

With this house Erskine offers a solution to two problems: whether one can build in a contemporary manner in historical surroundings if one undertakes to follow roof pitches and traditional grouping, as here with the house, studio, and garage; and, in addition, whether one can cope with buildings set in areas of large temperature variation.

Walls, floor and roof are of toughened foamed concrete slabs (Siporex). The wall slabs were poured in steel formwork and are untreated externally, and inside with dispersion colour.

Over the pitched roof (30 cm Siporex) lie sheets of galvanised corrugated steel black plastic coated (cold roof). Window surrounds are of mahogany, with frameless fixed sashes glazed with Thermopane, and have integral venetian blinds. External doors are of pine impregnated with black Solignum, with a lower cross-beam of teak.

House of the architect, R. Erskine, in Drottningholm

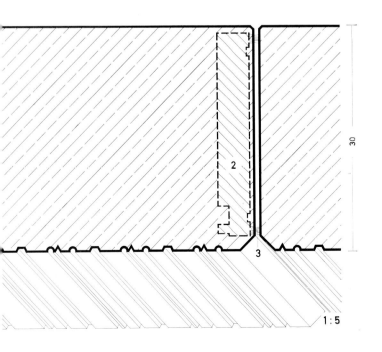

Concrete sandwich slabs

Factory for the firm Larsen and Nielson in Glostrup, Denmark

Prefabricated concrete wall slabs with a core of lightweight concrete. On the gable wall the external surface is exposed aggregate concrete with basalt stone facing. On the longitudinal walls it is a structural faced concrete.

The drawing shows a typical precast slab construction.

1 Reinforced concrete
2 Lightweight concrete (Leca)
3 Cramps 22 mm dia
4 Run off for condensation
5 Crane lugs (for lifting) 16 mm dia

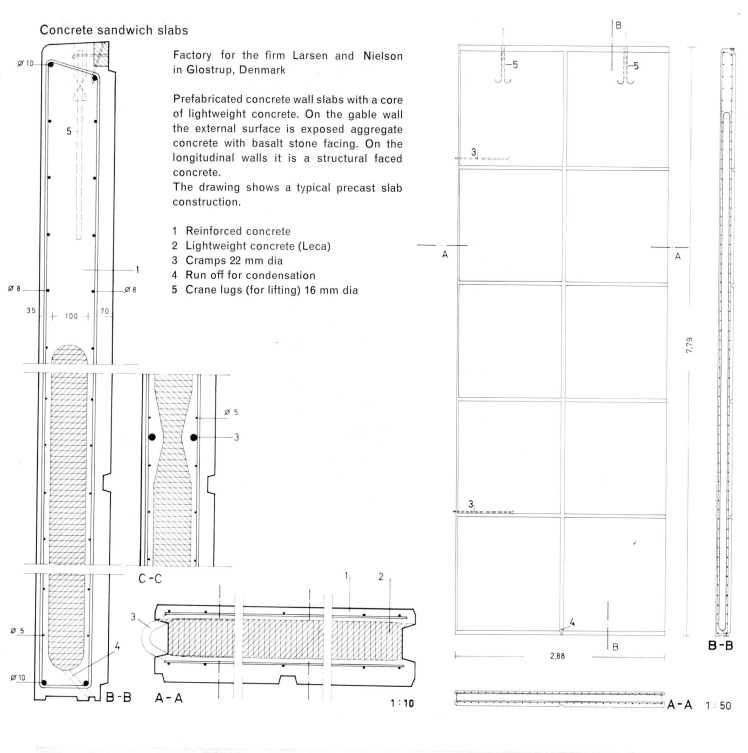

C-C

B-B   A-A   1:10

B-B

A-A   1:50

Factory and two storey extension of Varta AG, Hagen, Westphalia, Germany
Architect: Dr Ing Walter Heng, Braunschweig, in collaboration with Dr Ing L. Kammel

1 Anchor slots 28/15 mm
2 30/30/4 mm angles
3 Square section steel bar 15/10 mm
4 Durable mastic
5 U 3 100 cm long with hook head screw 118
6 Siporex sheets (GSB 35) 10 cm with groove
   33/33 mm
7 Back-up wall 11.5 cm brickwork

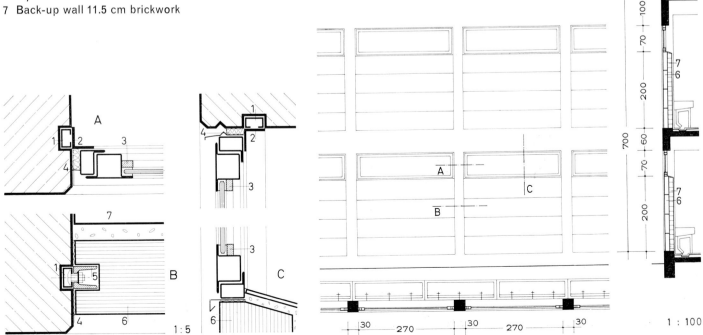

Sandwich panels in lightweight concrete

Above: Living quarters in Kiruna
Below: Housing estate in Svappara } both in Lapland, Sweden
Architect: Rolf Erskine, Drottningholm

In both cases the external walls are constructed of lightweight concrete sandwich panels.

Construction principles are similar to those on the opposite page.

The elements are about 50 cm wide, 256 cm high and 22.5 cm thick. They are painted externally in various tones of red and ochre. The heat insulation takes account of the situation of the buildings which are in fact north of the polar circle.

1 Face concrete untreated
2 Durable mastic joint sealer
3 Membrane
4 Foamed plastic insulation sheet
5 Insulation strips laid in and pressed on site
6 Dowel bar
7 Stirrup
8 Round steel bar
9 Grout mortar

Living quarters in Grüzefeld, Winterthur, Switzerland
Architects: Fred Cramer, Werner Jaray, Claude Paillard, Peter Leemann, Zurich; Hersteller Element AG, Veltheim

The total project consists of four different blocks of dwellings of 2 to 12 storeys. The construction elements are mostly storey height. For the external walls sandwich panels were used, which with a total thickness of only 21 cm have a K-value of 0.65 Kcal/m² H °C.

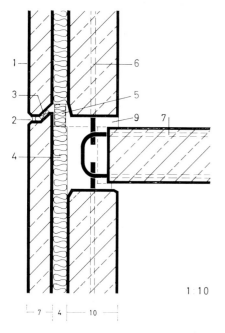

1 : 10

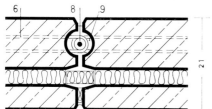

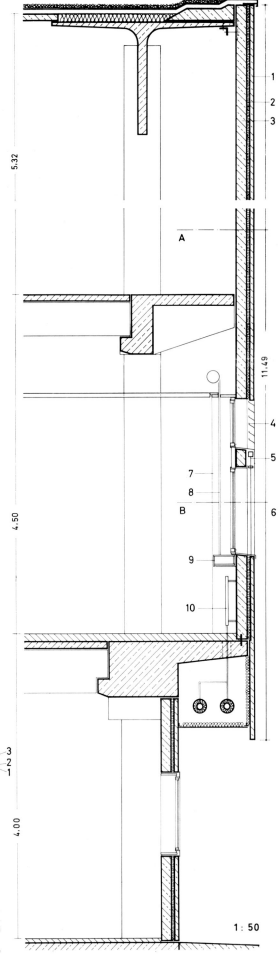

University of Stuttgart – Institute of Radiation Physics: Laboratory Hall for a 4 MeV-Dynamitron
Designed by the University Construction Faculty, Stuttgart: Adalbert Sack and Walter Tornack

Facade cladding is of sandwich slabs 2.5/11.4 cm. The 6 cm heavy exposed aggregate concrete outer skin of the sandwich panel is anchored to the bearing plate by 3.6 mm dia rustproof stirrups 6 per m². The slabs stand on the ground floor on the ring beam and are prevented from overturning by being fixed to the roof trusses.

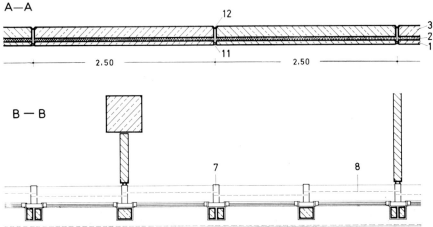

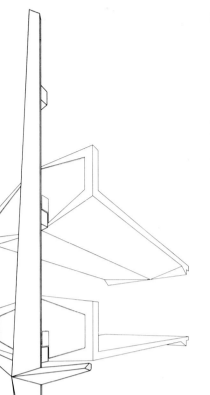

The assembly of the elements lasted 1 week and was carried out in the following order:

1 Assembly of the centre column and centre beam
2 Assembly of the external columns
3 Connection of the roof slabs with attached concrete parapet walls
4 Assembly of the beams on the narrow side of the flats
5 Pouring of the construction joints

Studio and flats in Düsseldorf
Architect: Walter Brune, Düsseldorf

The building presents a three storey facade to the street, with a fourth storey forming a garden at the lower level. With the exception of the staircases, it is formed of large section prefabricated concrete components. Formwork was of welded steel. Concrete components were auto-clave cured, without further treatment.

Total building time was 6 months.

Opposite details:
1 6 cm exposed aggregate concrete
2 3 cm polystyrene
3 15 cm reinforced concrete slab
4 Fixed aluminium louvres
5 Venetian blind
6 Aluminium pivot hung sash window
7 Columns, 2 mm steel sheet
8 Channels for anti-glare blind
9 Duct for high and low tension cables
10 Heating
11 Vacuum tube
12 Thiokol mastic on Neoprene gasket

Airport, Frankfurt am Main, simulator building
Architects: Apel, Beckert; Engineer: Becker, Frankfurt am Main

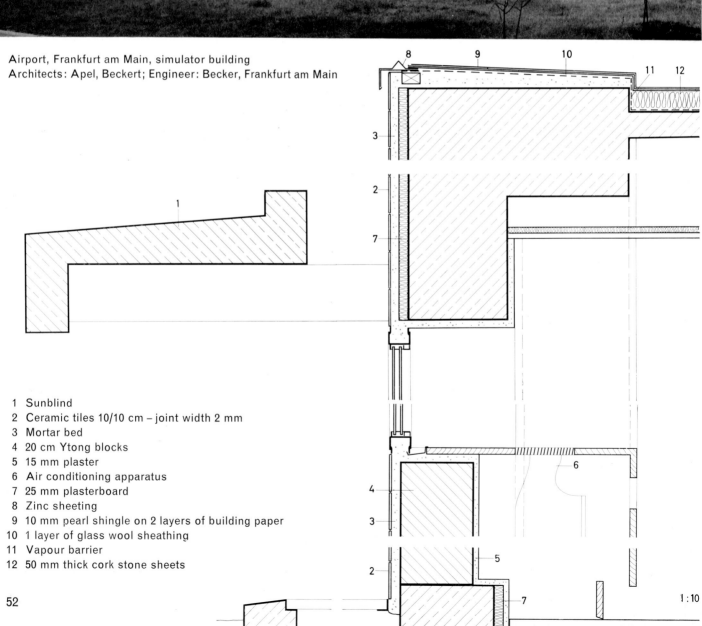

1 Sunblind
2 Ceramic tiles 10/10 cm – joint width 2 mm
3 Mortar bed
4 20 cm Ytong blocks
5 15 mm plaster
6 Air conditioning apparatus
7 25 mm plasterboard
8 Zinc sheeting
9 10 mm pearl shingle on 2 layers of building paper
10 1 layer of glass wool sheathing
11 Vapour barrier
12 50 mm thick cork stone sheets

1 : 10

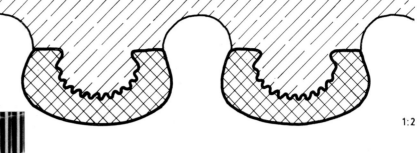

1:2

Town hall in Seinäjoki, Finland
Architects: Alvar Aalto, Helsinki, and Dr Leonardo Masso, Turin, Italy

Wall cladding in deep blue ceramic tiles 8.3/30 cm, designed by Aalto for this building and made in the porcelain factory Arabia in Helsinki. They are mortar bedded. The strong profile of the tiles is further expressed in the joints, the comparative surfaces are so large that in 1 sqm of wall surface more than 50% is joint surface area, and therefore there are no problems of damp staining behind the tiles. The tiles are 11 cm centre to centre. The joint width 6 cm.

1 25 cm insitu concrete
2 20 mm polystyrene
3 Aluminium foil
4 5 cm pumice slab
5 Plaster
6 Recess for service pipes fixed from storey to storey
7 Waterspout, copper U30/40/2 mm, concreted into wall slab
8 Balcony parapet precast on site, and used as shuttering for the balcony slab
9 25 mm dia steel pipe
10 Sheet covering, mortar bed laid to falls, Durban, cork on aluminium foil
11 Covering 3 mm, screed 35 mm, Sillan 25 mm
12 Covering 3 mm, reinforced screed 20 mm, cork 40 mm

High-rise housing in Lahr, Baden, Germany
Design: State Building Department, Freiburg, Germany

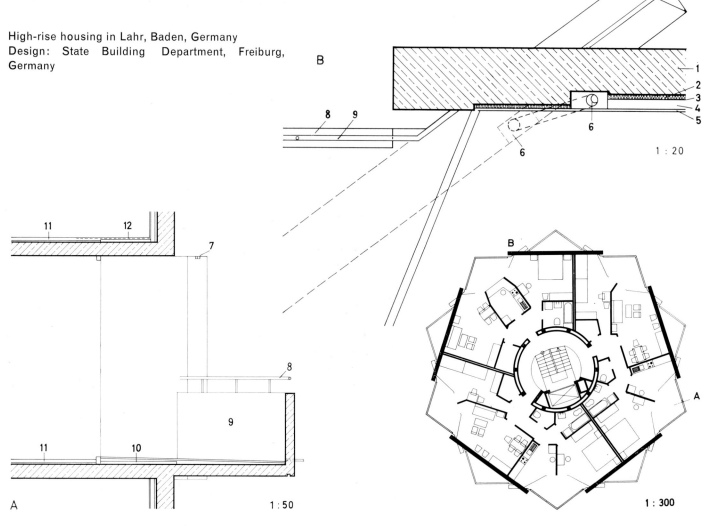

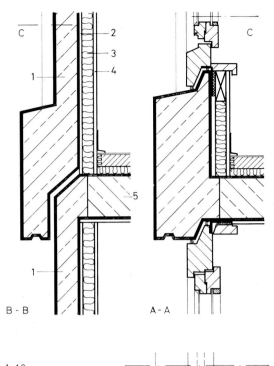

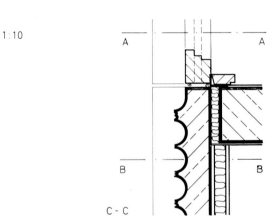

B - B   A - A

1:10

C - C

Block of flats in Sindelfingen, Germany
Architects: Peter Salzbrenner and Anton Schmidt, Stuttgart

1 Precast component   4 12 mm plasterboard
2 1 cm plaster   5 Insitu concrete
3 30 mm polystyrene

Structure of face concrete

Mechanically produced forms out of polystyrene, about 30 mm thick, were nailed to timber formwork and treated with a special separating film, so that they could remain in place as protection for the facade for the entire period in which the carcass was constructed. The special forms used for the precast components can be employed several times.

Right: Multi-family house in Biel, Switzerland
Left: A supporting wall in a street in Kanton Zürich, 130 m long, 2.55 m high.
Manufactured by PREWI in Winterthur, Switzerland. Similar forms are produced in Germany, eg: Fritz Seeger, Blankenloch, near Karlsruhe

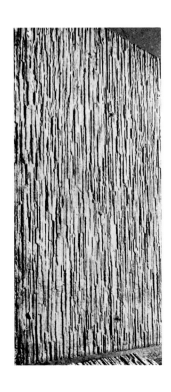

Blocks of high-rise flats in Chicago, Illinois, USA
Architect: Bertrand Goldberg Associates, Chicago

The two circular blocks are 30 m diameter and 18 storeys high. The other two are 58 m long and are 22 storeys high. Storey heights are 2.54 m.

The buildings are constructed with storey-height formwork elements made of plywood, embracing two of the bowed external surface elements. By using lightweight concrete and a thin wall thickness (externally 25.5 mm and internally 15.5 mm) the loading is kept to a minimum. The places where the bowed elements meet the abutting walls are considered as static supports and correspondingly reinforced. Also under these points are the pile foundations. For the lower six storeys lightweight concrete of higher strength was required. The walls are of consistent thickness in all storeys. Additional insulation was not necessary. Externally the elements are left rough from the formwork and are painted internally.

The windows have aluminium frames. The side panes are fixed glazed, the centre horizontal portion opens. Because of plastic insert gaskets, the window openings could only be concreted to a tolerance of 6 mm.

1 : 200

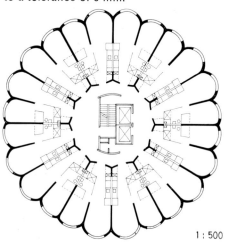

1 : 500

The external formwork consists of bowed plywood sheets with mastic sealing, stiffened with cross ribs (bracing), of 5/15 mm treated timber sections. A formwork element consists of two-storey high sections firmly fixed with the aid of scaffolding.

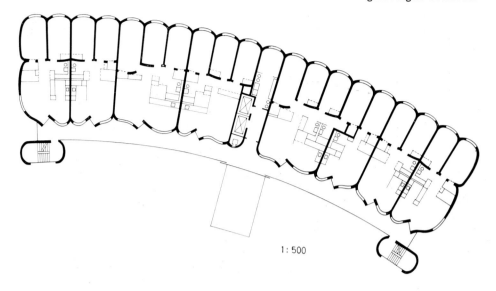

1 : 500

High-rise flats in Chicago   Architect: B. Goldberg Associates
Round the covered walkways the boarding is of unplaned planks

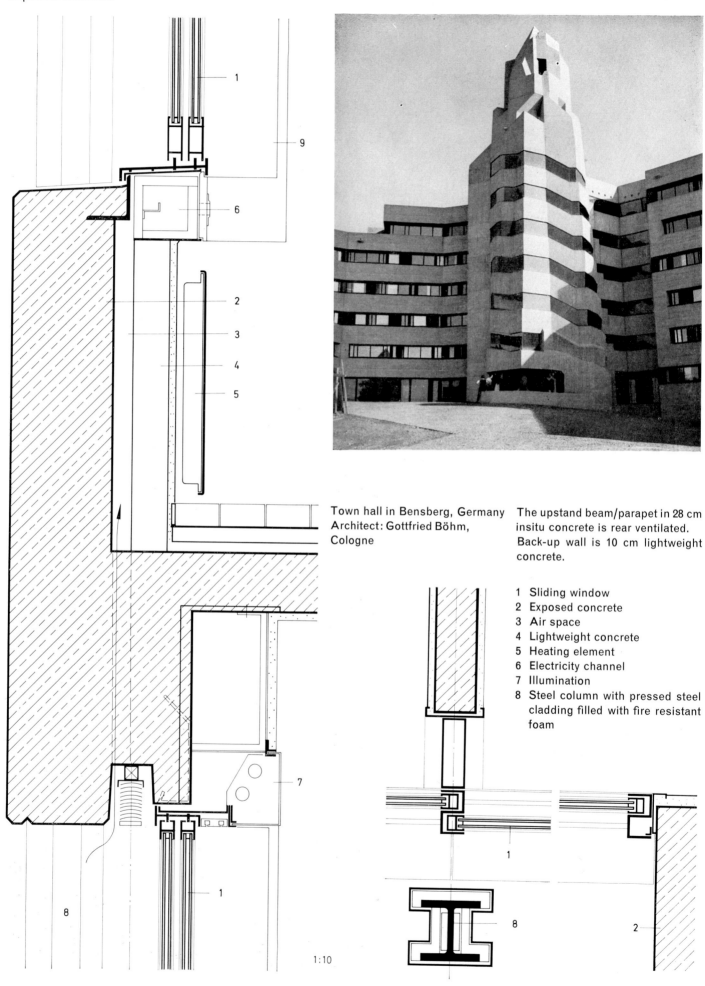

Town hall in Bensberg, Germany
Architect: Gottfried Böhm,
Cologne

The upstand beam/parapet in 28 cm
insitu concrete is rear ventilated.
Back-up wall is 10 cm lightweight
concrete.

1 Sliding window
2 Exposed concrete
3 Air space
4 Lightweight concrete
5 Heating element
6 Electricity channel
7 Illumination
8 Steel column with pressed steel
   cladding filled with fire resistant
   foam

1:10

High rise flats in Grenoble, France
Architects: R. H. Anger, Paris and Ch. Pivot, Grenoble, in collaboration
with P. Pucinelli

Exposed concrete painted white in parts. Insulated with foamed plastic
and back-up walls. Timber windows with double or triple glazing.

1:1000

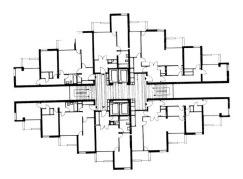

Exposed concrete

Church of St Paul's, Dielsdorf,
Switzerland
Architect: Dr Justus Dahinden,
Zürich

 1 Expanded concrete
 2 30 cm cork
 3 Waterproofed rendering
 4 Asbestos cement slates
 5 Gutter
 6 Rock wool mat
 7 Laminated purlin
 8 Larch ceiling soffit 16 mm
 9 120/62 mm steel column
10 Condensation channel
11 Purlin

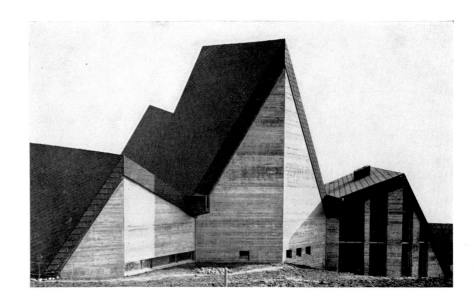

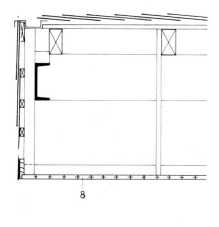

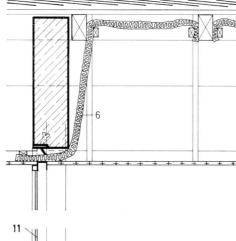

1 : 20

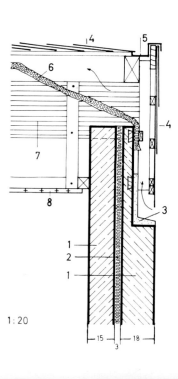

1 : 20

Church in St Gertrud, Cologne/Ehrenfeld,
Germany
Architect: Gottfried Böhm, Cologne

The external walls are 50 mm thick and have
fair faced concrete on both sides. A retard-
ing paste was spread on the formwork
boarding. After 12–36 hours the shuttering
was removed and after brushing out with a
wire brush, a surface similar to exposed
washed aggregate concrete was achieved.
No further heat insulation was necessary.
The church is heated by warmed air.

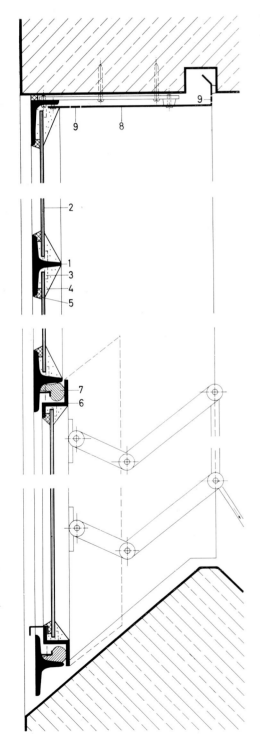

1 Main sashes of the windows out of
   T 80/40 mm sprayed ornamentally
2 Lead glazed areas
3 Glazing beads 30 cm
4 Steel window putty
5 Mastic putty

6 Ventilator frame
7 Rubber gasket held by brass screwed
   profile
8 Cladding of 2 mm galvanised steel
9 Ventilation 10 mm dia and 15 mm dia

1:5

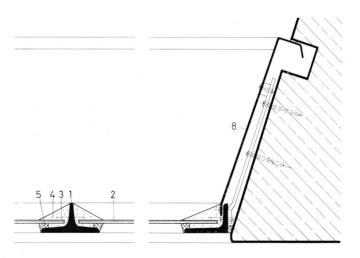

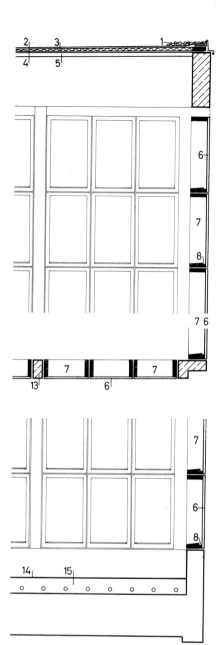

Church of Mary the Queen, Tuttlingen, Germany
Architects: F. J. Gottlich and M. W. Schraube, Tuttlingen

1 Gravel chippings covering
2 4 layers building paper
3 Granulated cork
4 1 layer building paper, perforated paper, aluminium Kraft
   paper
5 Pumice concrete planks
6 Glass concrete 3 cm
7 Concrete mullions – precast components
8 Condensation groove
9 Acrylic-based mastic joint sealer
10 Insulation
11 Grouting mortar
12 Cement mortar
13 Concrete column 25/15 cm (precast in two halves)
14 Marble slabs on pumice concrete
15 Underfloor heating

1 : 50

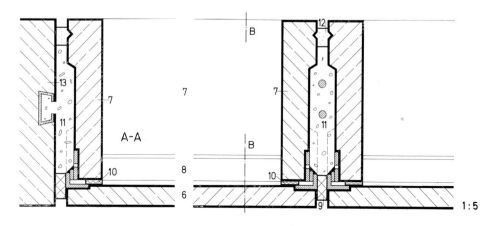

A-A

1 : 5

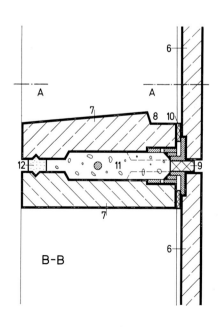

B-B

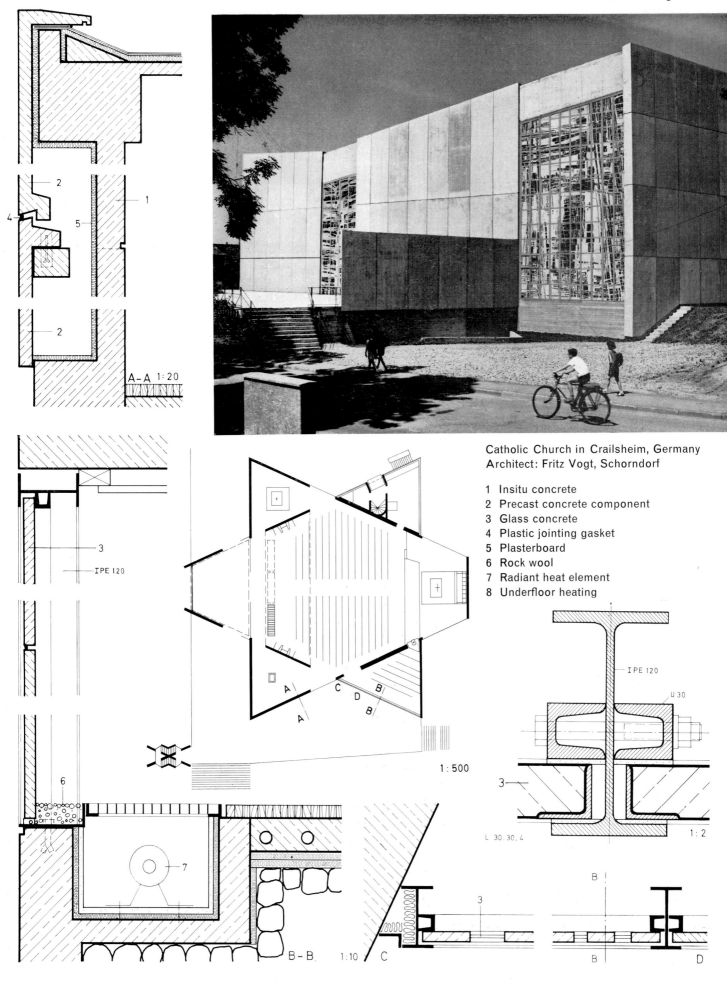

A–A 1:20

IPE 120

B–B. 1:10

Catholic Church in Crailsheim, Germany
Architect: Fritz Vogt, Schorndorf

1 Insitu concrete
2 Precast concrete component
3 Glass concrete
4 Plastic jointing gasket
5 Plasterboard
6 Rock wool
7 Radiant heat element
8 Underfloor heating

1:500

IPE 120

U 30

L 30.30.4

1:2

C

B–B

D

Concrete bricks

Cemetery chapel in Wermelskirchen, Germany
Architect: Friedrich Göbel, Wermelskirchen

Both walls of light ornamental concrete bricks designed by sculptor Eric Kuhn. The bricks have external glazing rebates into which the glass is puttied. The surrounding groove accepts, like a normal glass brick, the reinforcement of the joint.

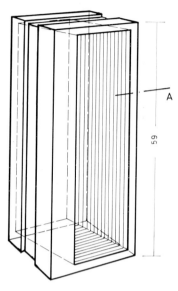

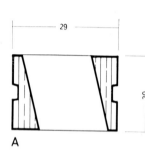

A

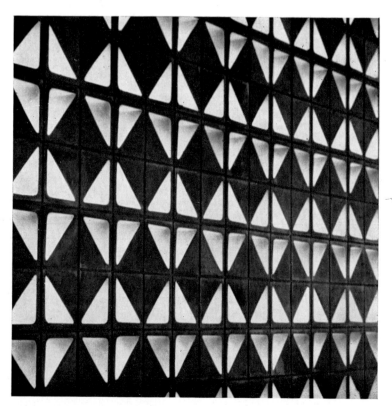

Evangelist Church in Völlinghausen on the Möhnesee, Germany
Architect: Rainer Mumme, Lippstadt

1 : 10

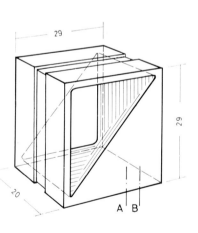

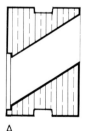

A

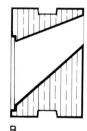

B

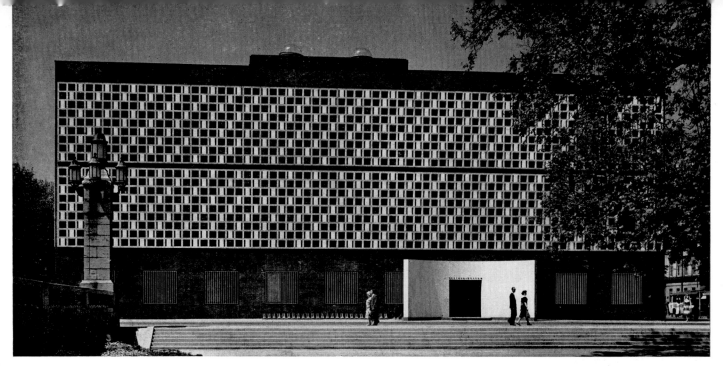

Kestner Museum in Hanover. Design: Building Construction Office, Hanover; Project management: Dierschke

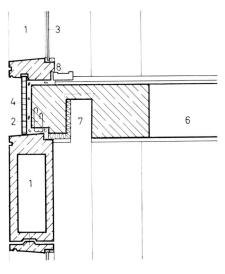

In extending the museum, the historical building remains as the kernel inside the new facade.

The ground floor, the first floor slab edging, and the roof parapet are covered with basalt pumice slabs. The entrance is in white marble.

1 Precast concrete components
2 Steel stirrup carried over the joints of the precast components
3 Thermopane with light reflecting class
4 Basalt pumice slabs
5 Exposed concrete column 27 cm dia
6 RC ribbed roof slabs
7 Recess for venetian blind
8 Condensation groove

1 : 500

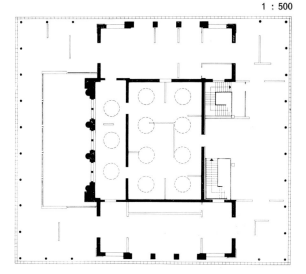

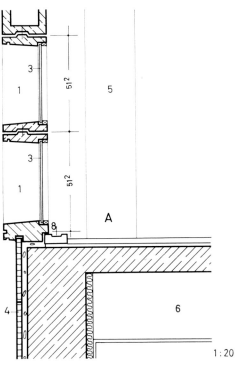

1 : 20

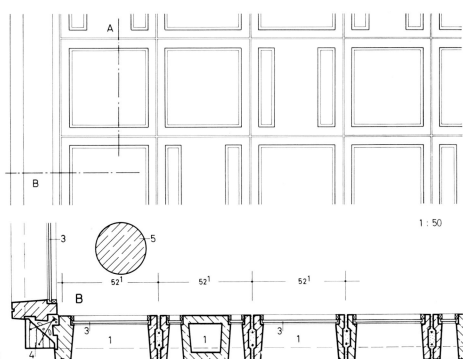

1 : 50

5

Glass bricks

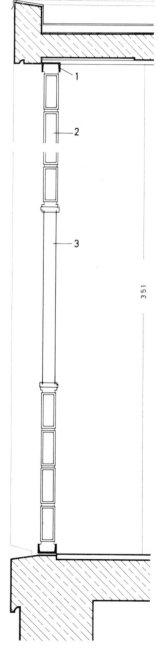

Printing works in Stuttgart-Vaihingen
Architect: R. Wacker, Zürich
Building Contractor: Erwin Becker, Stuttgart

1 Surrounding frames U 10
2 Glass bricks 20/20/8 cm
3 Ventilation window
4 Expansion joint with inset hard foam strips
5 Bitumen paper
6 Mastic putty

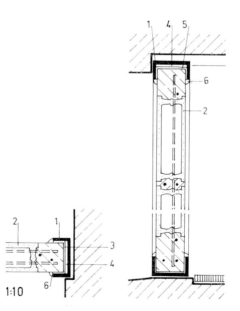

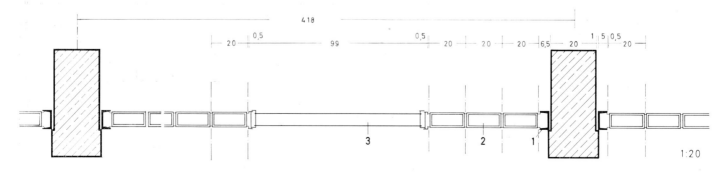

Free University, Berlin: Library tower
Architects: F. H. Sobotka and G. Müller, Berlin

The tower has ten storeys. Floor heights 237 cm, illuminated room space 217 cm. Sizes of the glass bricks: 14 cm wide, 245 cm high, joint width, horizontal 76 mm, vertical 55 mm. Overall dimension of the glass brick area: 258 cm wide, 217 cm high.

Process hall for a rolling mill in Weidenau, Hüttental, Germany

The hall is of steel skeleton construction. The facade is infilled with Schalker glass bricks 19/19/8 cm. Total length of the glazed surface 127 m, height 8.5 m. Overall dimension of one glass brick panel 3.10 m wide, 4.20 m high.

Crystallized glass

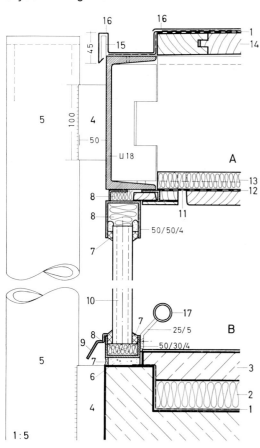

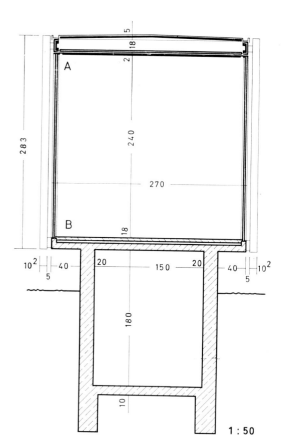

1 Bitumen paper
2 Perlite
3 Anhydrite screed
4 Iron clamp
5 Pipe dia 102/10 mm
6 Mortar
7 Duralin/Duroflex mastic
8 Micro glass wool
9 Weather mould apron
10 Crystallized glass construction element
11 Air space
12 Woven nylon or porous foil
13 Rock wool
14 T & G boarding 30 mm
15 Sheet steel gutter and trim 20/5 cm
16 Copper sheet roof covering
17 Spur post – gas pipe 25 mm dia

Roofed connecting passage, Psychiatric County Hospital, Weinsberg, Germany
Architect: Werner Gabriel, Stuttgart

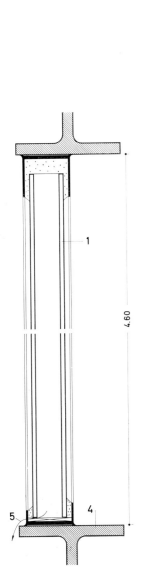

Printing works for the *Corriere della Sera*, Milan, Italy
Architects: Gio Ponti, Antonio Fornoroli and Albert Roselli, Milan
Planning: Albert Roselli

1 Profilit construction glass 25/4 cm
2 Aluminium opening lights
3 Steel column IPB 360
4 Steel column IPE 360
5 Condensation drainage outlet 6 mm dia, all 50 cm

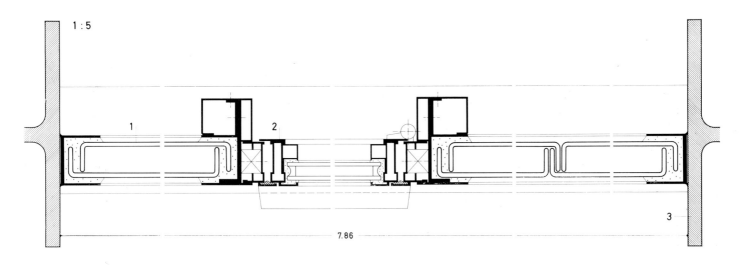

1 : 5

5 *

Opposite: Oxford Centre
for Management Studies,
England: Students hostel
Architects: Peter Ahrends,
Richard Burton, Paul
Koralek, London

Otsuma secondary school for girls, Tokyo: Library △
Design: Nikken Senkei Ltd, Osaka, Japan
Planning: Kazumasa Yamashita and Yasuo Tadano, Tokyo

Behind the dormer windows of the upper five floors are classrooms. The roofs of the dormers are clear wired glass 6/8 mm
thick. The opening windows are of 5 mm plate glass. Sun
protection from half mirrored polythene foil roller blinds. The
window frames and the water outlets between the dormers,
as well as the rain water pipes, are of natural anodised aluminium. The concrete walls were sprayed silver.

The bedsitting rooms are linked in maisonette form. By raking
the windows the glass surface is enlarged, and the light will
penetrate to the rear of the room. The construction of the
windows from outside to inside is as follows:

(a) fixed 2-pane safety glass 6 mm thick, frameless on the lower
    edge and fixed only at the corners to permit run off of water
(b) venetian blinds
(c) inside window is a single glazed hopper type with an alu-
    minium frame
(d) roller sun blinds.

The underlying narrow window has an aluminium frame and
acts as a ventilation hopper.
Profiles and edges are protected with zinc sheet. The wall
surfaces are covered with waterproofed plywood and zinc sheet.
Frame sockets in exposed concrete are of calcium silicate
bricks.

Pimlico School, London
Design: Inner Education Authority, Department of Architecture and Civic Design, London. Head: Sir Hubert Bennett
Education Architect: Michael Powell
Group Leader: John Bancroft

The school is in the heart of London. By staggering the storeys, the windows to the classrooms can be carried over the roof, thereby achieving good daylight penetration into the classrooms.
Roof glazing is 5 mm plate glass and 6 mm ornamental wired glass. Between the panels are 12 mm PVC foamed slabs.
Windows are glazed with 12 mm mirror glass. Window frames are of anodised aluminium natural colour, and the surrounds of softwood stained dark brown. Sun protection on the south and west sides by plastic roller blinds and additional air conditioning in the classrooms on the south side. The load bearing external wall is in exposed concrete.

All-glass wall

Car showroom, Paris
Architect: Jean de Mailly, Paris
Originator of the all-glass wall: La Société Française du Verre, Drancy

The folded glass front was manufactured out of 140 cm wide glass sheets, 10-12 mm thick. The middle door consists of two 2-sectioned folding doors, their middle section serving the flow of public traffic. To allow lorries to pass the 4 sections open, as does the upper area.

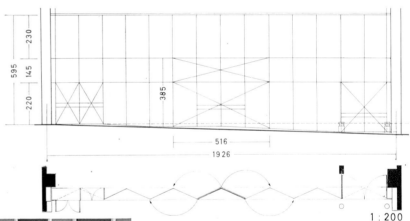

1 : 200

Design Research Headquarters in Cambridge, Massachusetts, USA
Architects: Benjamin Thompson & Associates, Cambridge, Massachusetts

The strong emphasis of the structural system amplifies the external surface which is wholly of glass. Apart from the service core there are no internal walls within the storeys, and this emphasises still further the feeling of transparency, especially at night when the building appears as one huge shop window. In order to maintain this impression, the full name of the firm was not put on a fascia, and instead a single reference to the firm, DR (Design Research) in narrow orange/red neon letters, is mounted in the space behind the glass facade.
The glass surfaces are single pane safety glass of 9-10 mm thickness, 240 cm high and 150 cm wide are frameless and puttied into grooves in the concrete. The grooves are 3.8 cm wide, below 3.8 cm, above 6.5 cm high. The vertical corners are butted obliquely together, and sealed and fixed with two stainless steel clamps. The sealer is a translucent silicon mastic. The slab edges and soffits are in sand faced exposed concrete.

All-glass wall

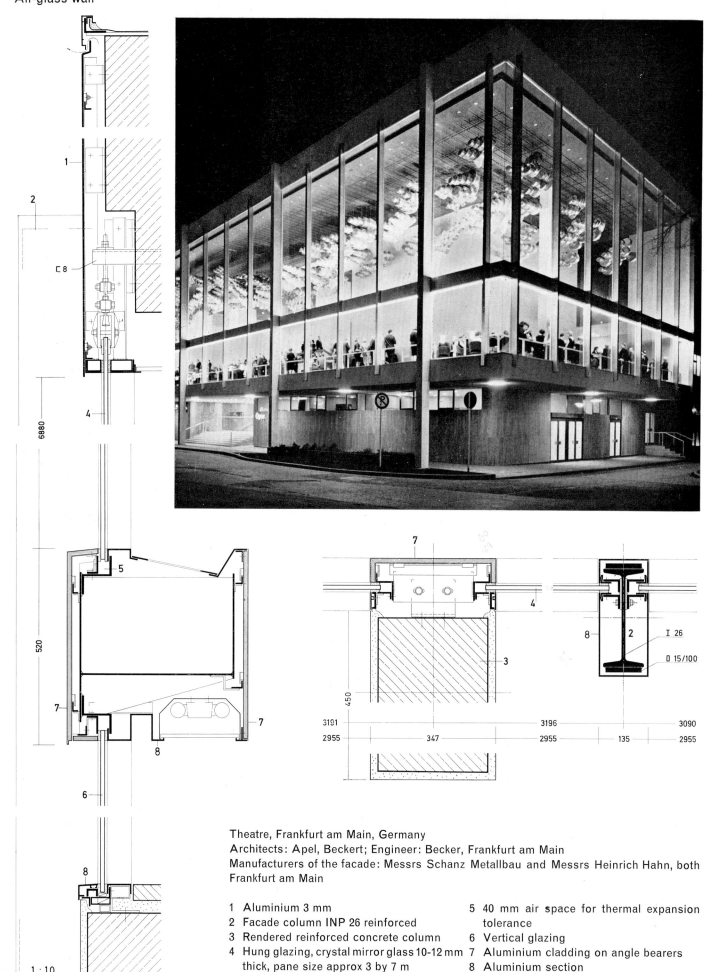

Theatre, Frankfurt am Main, Germany
Architects: Apel, Beckert; Engineer: Becker, Frankfurt am Main
Manufacturers of the facade: Messrs Schanz Metallbau and Messrs Heinrich Hahn, both
Frankfurt am Main

1 Aluminium 3 mm
2 Facade column INP 26 reinforced
3 Rendered reinforced concrete column
4 Hung glazing, crystal mirror glass 10-12 mm
   thick, pane size approx 3 by 7 m
5 40 mm air space for thermal expansion
   tolerance
6 Vertical glazing
7 Aluminium cladding on angle bearers
8 Aluminium section

1 : 10

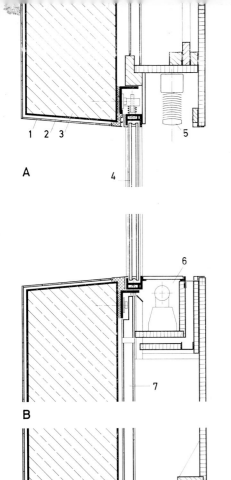

A

B

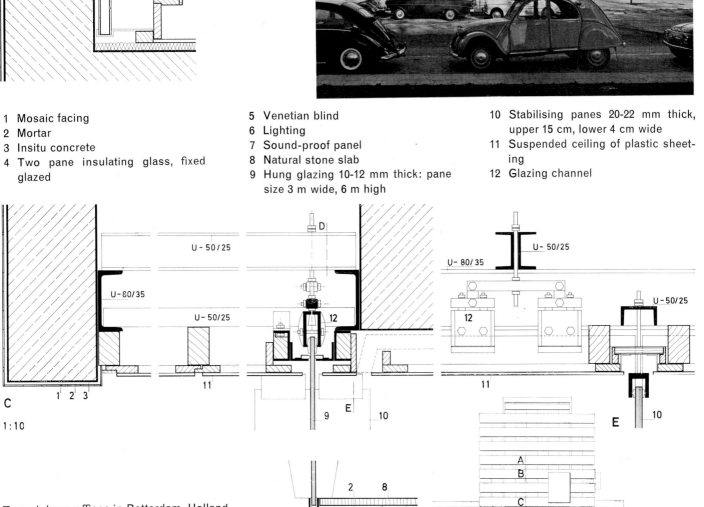

1 Mosaic facing
2 Mortar
3 Insitu concrete
4 Two pane insulating glass, fixed glazed

5 Venetian blind
6 Lighting
7 Sound-proof panel
8 Natural stone slab
9 Hung glazing 10-12 mm thick: pane size 3 m wide, 6 m high

10 Stabilising panes 20-22 mm thick, upper 15 cm, lower 4 cm wide
11 Suspended ceiling of plastic sheeting
12 Glazing channel

C

1:10

D

E

1:1000

Tomadohaus offices in Rotterdam, Holland
Architects: Maaskant, van Dommelen, Kroos, Senf, Rotterdam

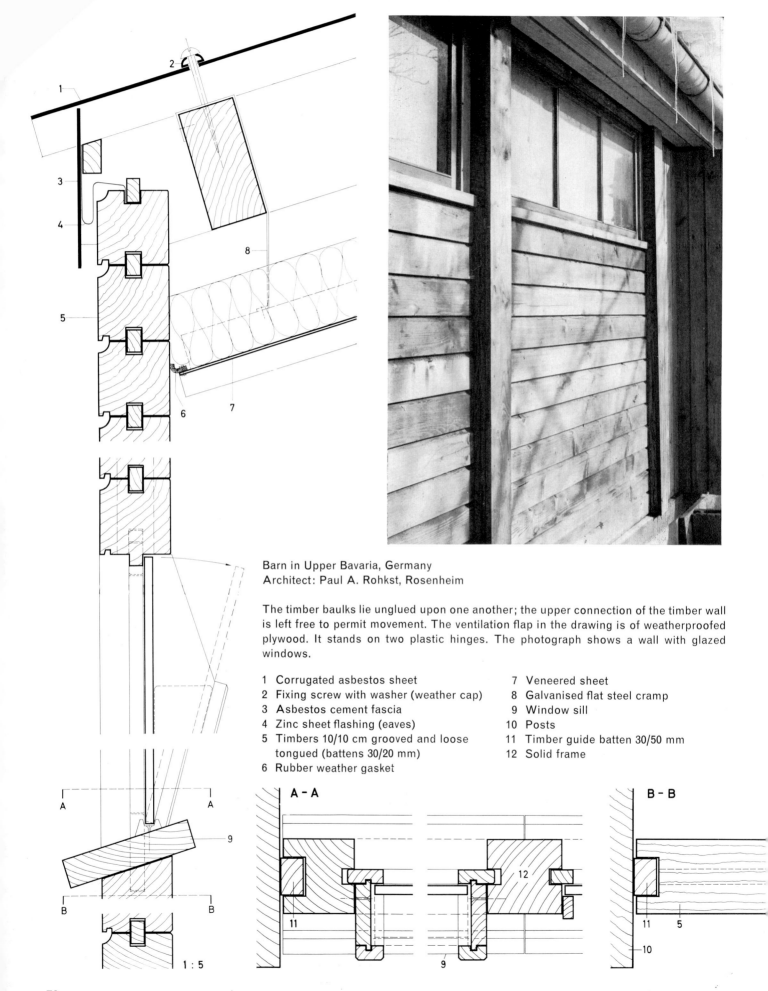

Barn in Upper Bavaria, Germany
Architect: Paul A. Rohkst, Rosenheim

The timber baulks lie unglued upon one another; the upper connection of the timber wall is left free to permit movement. The ventilation flap in the drawing is of weatherproofed plywood. It stands on two plastic hinges. The photograph shows a wall with glazed windows.

1 Corrugated asbestos sheet
2 Fixing screw with washer (weather cap)
3 Asbestos cement fascia
4 Zinc sheet flashing (eaves)
5 Timbers 10/10 cm grooved and loose tongued (battens 30/20 mm)
6 Rubber weather gasket
7 Veneered sheet
8 Galvanised flat steel cramp
9 Window sill
10 Posts
11 Timber guide batten 30/50 mm
12 Solid frame

A – A

B – B

1 : 5

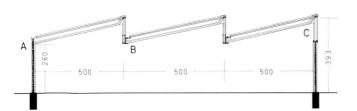

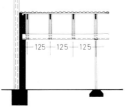

1 : 200

Solid timber

1 Logs approx 7 cm dia
2 Glued frame 8/18 cm
3 Glass wool 5 cm covered both sides with bitumen paper
4 Soffit boards 62.5/125 cm, 19 mm thick
5 Glass wool mat 5 cm
6 Glued truss 8/26 cm, spacing 1.5 m

7 Oregon pine boarding
8 Corrugated asbestos sheeting
9 Building paper
10 Spandrel cover sheet of GRP approx 2 cm thick, transparent
11 Ventilation of the roof space
12 Valley gutter of rigid PVC

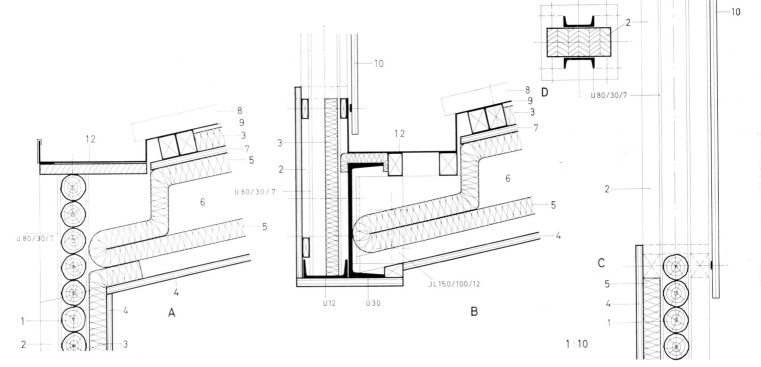

A

B

1 : 10

C

D

U 80/30/7

Presberg farm: Barn of prefabricated components
Architect: Karl Wilhelm Schüssler, Zürich-Thalwil

Single family house in Syosset, NY, USA
Architect: Anthony Ellner Jnr, Tempe, Arizona

Pure timber construction. The wall panels, approx 2.3 m high, are either of timber or glazed (sliding doors with aluminium frames). A continuous clerestory separates them from the roof construction which is of thick planking in folded plate form.

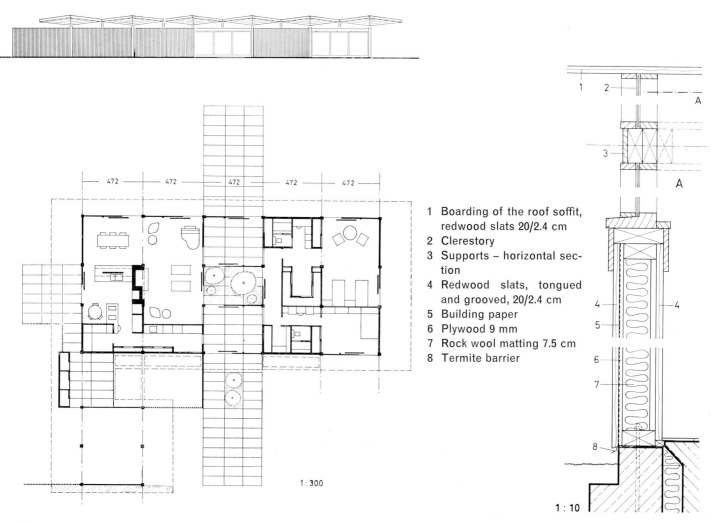

1 : 300

1 Boarding of the roof soffit, redwood slats 20/2.4 cm
2 Clerestory
3 Supports – horizontal section
4 Redwood slats, tongued and grooved, 20/2.4 cm
5 Building paper
6 Plywood 9 mm
7 Rock wool matting 7.5 cm
8 Termite barrier

1 : 10

Church of Christ, Portola Valley, California, USA
Architects: Clark & Beuttler, San Francisco

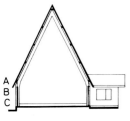

1 Hand-split cedar shingles 60 cm long, up to 15 cm wide
2 Tongued and grooved boarding 5 cm hemlock
3 Fly screen
4 Shutter, 24 mm redwood
5 Transomes 7.5/20 cm redwood
6 Coloured cast glass
7 Wall area of 2 framed timbers 5/10 cm, braces 5/10 cm, all at 60 cm, redwood cladding 24 mm
8 Continuous sill member
9 Limed frame members 40/14 cm Douglas fir, stained red
10 Gable wall of double timbers 5/20 cm, brace timbers all 60 cm. Cladding 24 mm redwood, externally on diagonal boarding

1 : 500

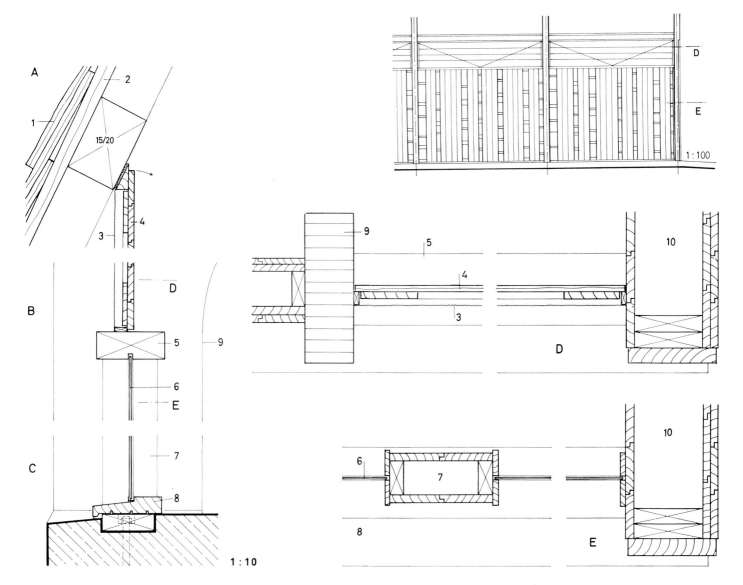

1 : 100

1 : 10

Weekend house in Aeschlen, Switzerland
Architect: Werner Küenzi, Bern

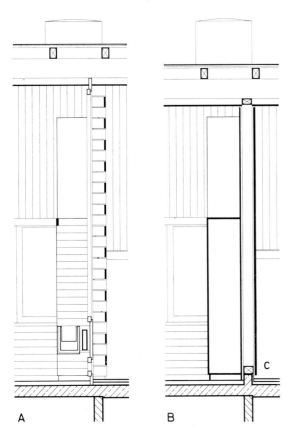

A

B

1 Reinforced concrete
2 Cork 20 mm
3 Insulation mat
4 Cement screed 40 mm
5 Fitted carpet
6 Base board
7 Boarding 110/16 mm on 25 mm battens
8 Boarding 160/24 mm
9 Rock wool mat
10 Diagonal boarding 30 mm
11 Wind porch
12 Kitchen
13 Living room
14 Open fireplace
15 Flower trough
16 Cupboard
17 Working space
18 Car port

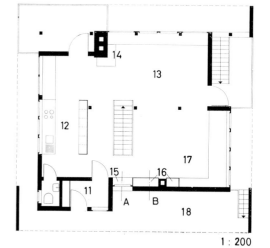

1 : 200

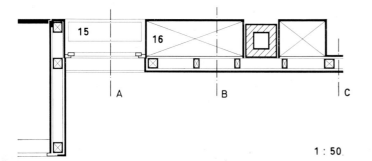

1 : 50

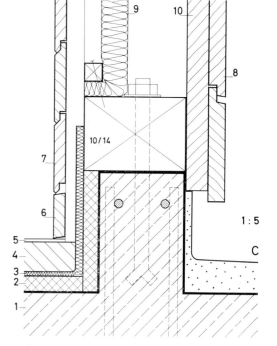

1 : 5

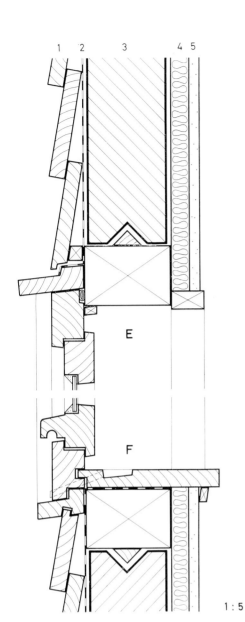

Lobster hut on Helgoland
Architect: George Wellhausen, Hamburg

The separating walls are of concrete and at the same time serve as support for the rear retaining wall. The huts serve as storerooms.

1 Scots pine ship lap boarding 150/22 mm, planed
2 Tar paper
3 Inner wall 11.5 cm
4 Plasterboard 25 mm
5 Plaster skim coat 15 cm

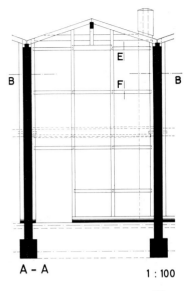

A – A   1 : 100

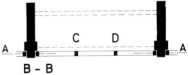

B – B

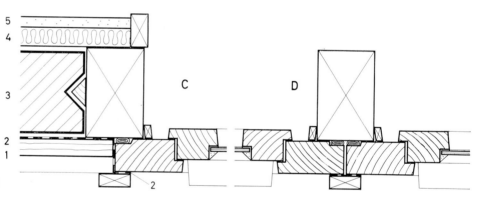

1 : 5

Board cladding

Single family house in Mercer Island,
Washington, USA
Architect: Wendell H. Lovett, Bellevue,
Washington

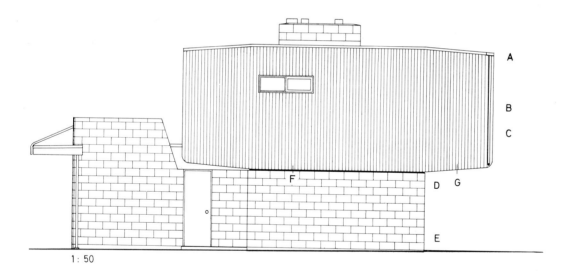

1 : 50

1 Aluminium
2 Triple layer felted roof
3 Plywood 12 mm
4 Roof beams of two timbers 5/15 cm
5 Plywood 9 mm
6 Roofing felt
7 Cedar horizontal cladding
8 Timber framing 5/10 cm
9 Cedar vertical cladding 18 mm
10 Pumice stone, facing to insitu concrete, painted white

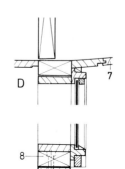

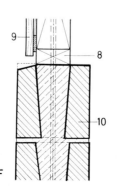

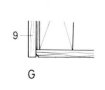

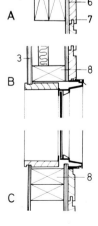

1 : 10

Balcony access housing in Tibro, Sweden
Architect: Ralf Erskine, Drottningholm

The external walls are of lightweight concrete (Siporex) rendered in the ground storey, the upper storeys are clad in spruce ship lapped boarding timber section 5/5 cm. The infill timbers in the balcony parapets are of the same section. They are screwed to the vertical timber frames leaving a gap of approx 15 mm between the timbers. The cladding and parapet, and entrance doors, are impregnated with black and red Solignum respectively. The balcony framing timbers are 7/30 cm cross section, and are of natural wrought timber. The load bearing frames of the balconies are of precast exposed concrete components.

Timber cladding

Refectory of the University of Leicester, England
Architects: Richard Shepherd, Robson & Partners, London

Above: Cross section through the refectory showing the kitchen behind.

Below: Longitudinal section: the timber cladding is carried over the adjoining building to the right.

Opposite:
1 Aluminium sheet
2 Lead water check
3 Puttyless glazing
4 3 layers of felt
5 Cedar cladding 240/20 cm
6 Felt backing sheet
7 Rough sawn supports all approx 60 cm
8 Glass fibre faced with cardboard
9 Painted boarding 220/20 mm
10 Steel columns NP 20 lacquered black all approx 6 m
11 Sliding door
12 Fixed glazing
13 Felt strip
14 Cedar timber window

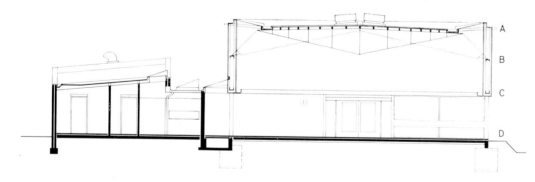

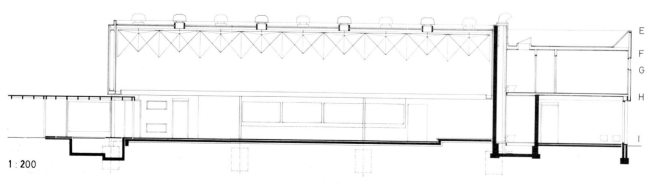

1 : 200

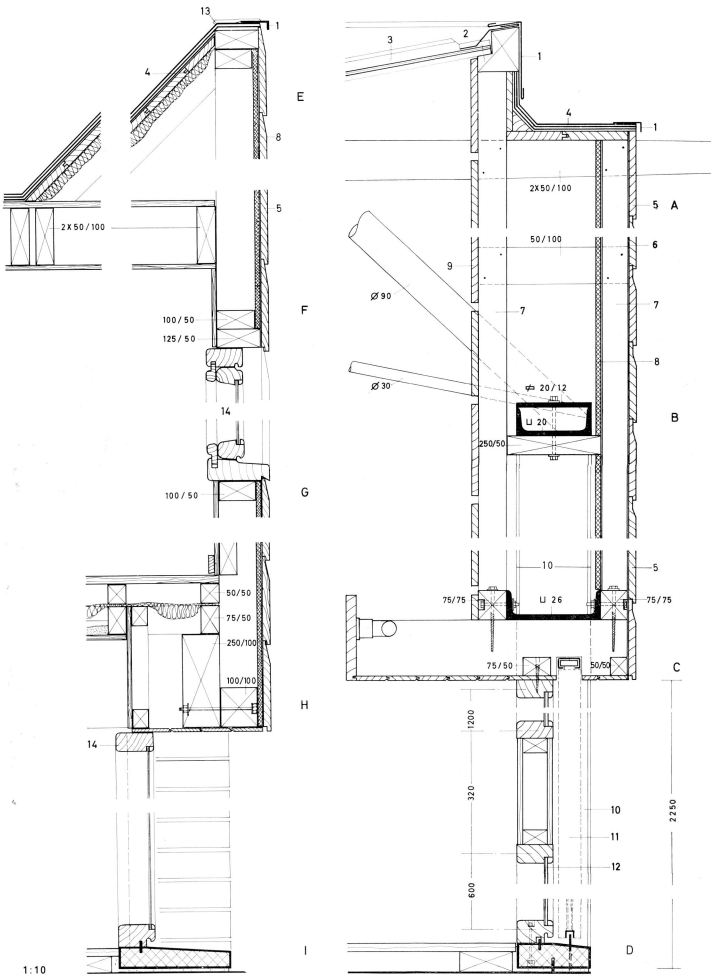

13

1

4

E

8

3

2

1

5 A

2X50/100

F

5

2X50/100

100/50

125/50

14

G

100/50

6

9

Ø90

7

7

Ø30

8

20/12

B

⊔20

250/50

H

50/50

75/50

250/100

100/100

14

I

1:10

10

5

75/75

⊔26

75/75

75/50

50/50

C

1200

320

10

11

12

600

2250

D

Single family house on the beach in Sagaponac, Long Island, NY, USA
Architect: Norman Jaffe, New York, in collaboration with Michael Wolfe

Hand split shingles (shakes) of red cedar, 46 cm long, 14 cm exposed, lower part 3.8 cm thick, thin end 1.6 cm thick.

Two storey group of flats in Portland, Oregon, USA
Architects: William Martin and David A. Soderstrom, Portland

Sawn shingles of red cedar, 40 cm long, 13 cm exposed, minimum width 7.5 cm, minimum thickness 10 mm.

The walls are of timber framing, mineral wool insulation, covered with 13 mm waterproofed plywood and a layer of Kraft paper. The shingles are secured with rust proofed nails.

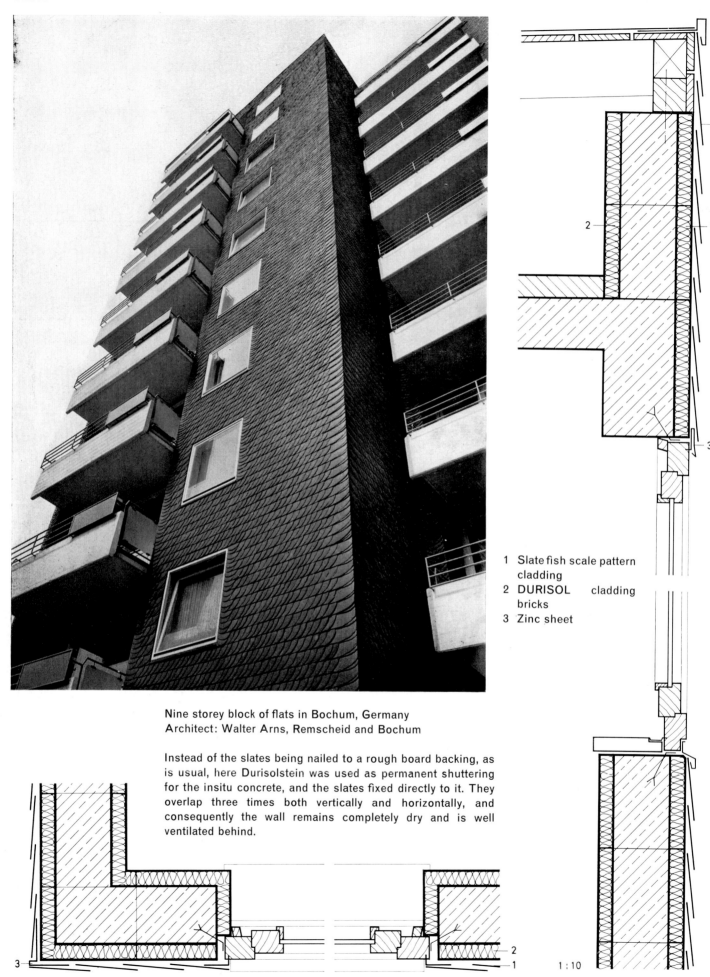

Nine storey block of flats in Bochum, Germany
Architect: Walter Arns, Remscheid and Bochum

Instead of the slates being nailed to a rough board backing, as is usual, here Durisolstein was used as permanent shuttering for the insitu concrete, and the slates fixed directly to it. They overlap three times both vertically and horizontally, and consequently the wall remains completely dry and is well ventilated behind.

1 Slate fish scale pattern cladding
2 DURISOL cladding bricks
3 Zinc sheet

1 : 10

Bungalow in the Ruhr area, Germany
Architect: Walter Arns, Remscheid and Bochum

Wall cladding is of slates laid in fish scale pattern. The construction is similar to the block of flats on the opposite page.

Details of the slate cladding from the Moselle slate manufacturing firm, J. B. Rathscheck & Sons KG, Mayen

Above: English cladding. Architect: Fellen, Cologne-Stammheim
Right: Irregular coursed fish scale cladding

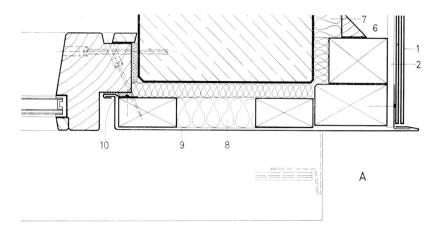

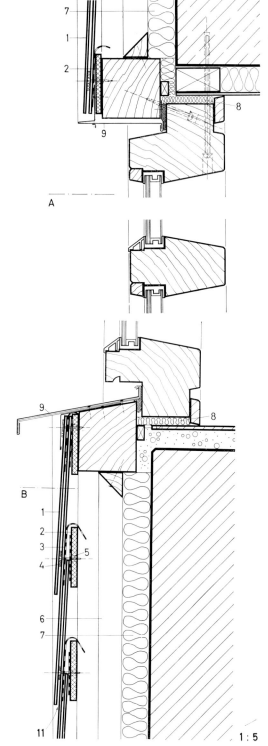

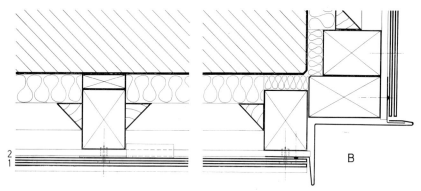

District hospital Simbach, Inn
Architects: Werner Eichberg and Otto Roth, Munich

1 Asbestos cement slates 30/50 cm
2 Eternite fillet
3 Roofing felt 8/8 cm
4 Plastic washer
5 Plastic plug
6 Air space
7 Plasterboard 35 mm
8 Glass wool
9 Aluminium 1.5 mm
10 Compressible strip
11 Ventilation

Catholic church in Hüttwilen, Switzerland
Architect: Dr Justus Dahinden, Zürich, in collaboration with Peter Banholzer

Walls and roof are covered with black Eternite slates. Slate size on the church 30/60 cm, overlapping according to the pitch 8 to 12 cm. Slate size on the tower 30/40 cm in English double coursing, fixed with the usual hooks and in every case the top course is nailed to the ridge. The edges are protected with chamfered copper sheeting. The sheets extend at the sides under the penultimate Eternite sheets and are completely covered by the last one.
Construction: Glued trusses and rafters overlaid with Eternite sheets (Gea-Unterdach) then battens and counter battens for fixing the cladding. Insulating quilting laid between the rafters. Internal cladding is larch boarding.

Asbestos cement sheets

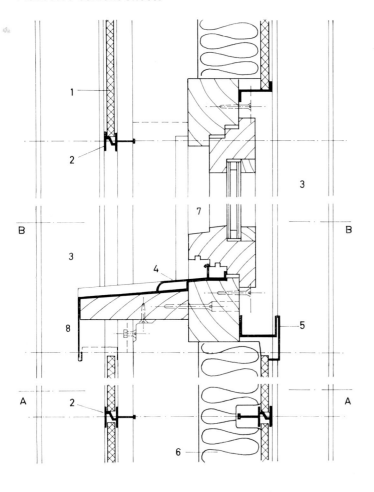

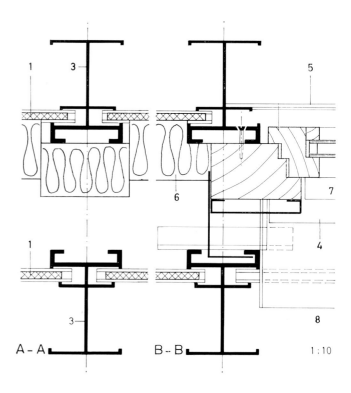

A-A   B-B   1:10

1 Asbestos cement sheets 12 mm
2 Cross section
3 Main supports 20/28 cm
4 Rain protection strip
5 Condensation channel
6 Mineral wool sheet 80 mm
7 Timber window with sealed insulating glass
8 Sheet metal sill covering

Weaving factory in Sirnach, Switzerland
Architects: F. Stäheli and H. Frehner, St Gallen

The ground floor is constructed of reinforced concrete. The wall construction for the factory is of aluminium infilled with grey asbestos cement sheets, 12 mm thick. The wall is built in two-skin cavity form with a fully ventilated cavity space approx 12 cm wide.
The mineral wool on the external face of the inner wall was stuck on before assembly of the Eternite sheets. The wall construction has a patent pending.

Housing group on the Opernplatz, Berlin, Architect: Rolf Gutbrod, Stuttgart and Berlin, in collaboration with Sigbert Vogt, Horst Schwaderer and Rainer Franzmann

The block stands in Charlottenburg in the centre of Berlin. On the ground floor and partially encroaching into the first floor are shops and restaurants, above are five to thirteen storey flats.

The construction is a reinforced concrete shell, the outer walls clad with pumice concrete 24 cm thick, covered with steam cured asbestos cement sheets 8 mm thick, fixed to 30 mm thick timber battens. The battens lie in every case behind the joints of the sheets.

The horizontal joints are sealed. Joint width 10 mm.

Batten width 70 mm. Horizontal joints 30 mm wide, batten width 100 mm. Maximum size of the sheets 2.75/1.25 m. For drips and external corners curved form pieces were used.

Exposed aggregate concrete panels

Postal cheque service and giro counter in The Hague,
Holland
Architects: J. H. van den Broek and J. B. Bakema,
Rotterdam

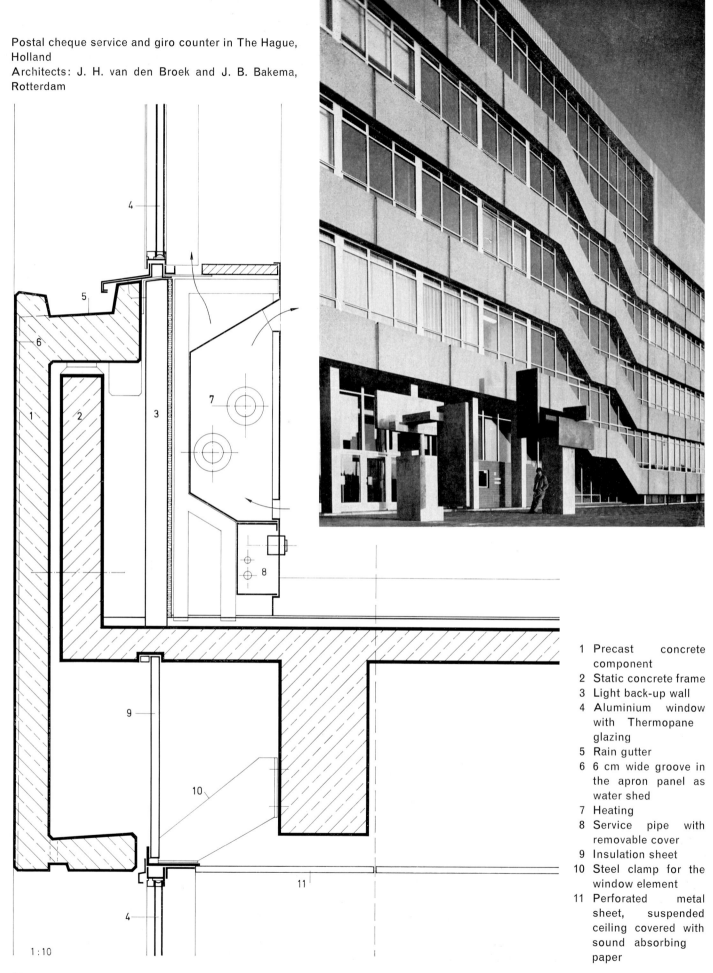

1 Precast concrete component
2 Static concrete frame
3 Light back-up wall
4 Aluminium window with Thermopane glazing
5 Rain gutter
6 6 cm wide groove in the apron panel as water shed
7 Heating
8 Service pipe with removable cover
9 Insulation sheet
10 Steel clamp for the window element
11 Perforated metal sheet, suspended ceiling covered with sound absorbing paper

1:10

Rehabilitation centre in Madrid
Architect: Dr Miguel Fisac, Madrid

Large scale concrete slabs as rear ventilated wall cladding

The base structure for the preformed concrete elements is of horizontal, vertical and cross braced steel wires. The triangular area thus formed should not be greater than 2500 cm². The tensioned wires (in other cases also wire mesh) provide maximum surface areas of 100 cm². The forms were lined with polyethylene sheet and the concrete poured into the mould. Because of the elasticity of the formwork sheet and the small displacement of the wires the elements were similar but not completely identical.

Concrete panels with ceramic cladding

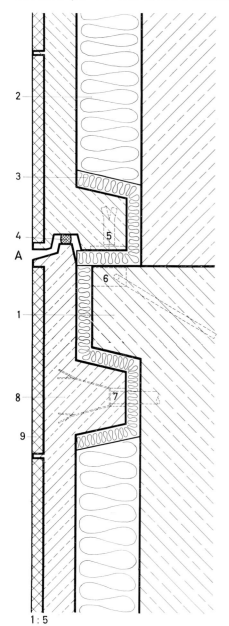

1 : 5

Tower block on the Wiener Platz, Cologne
Architect: Karl Hell, Cologne

1 Insitu concrete 15 cm
2 Polystyrene 90 mm
3 Frigolith 20 mm
4 Plasticised joint filler
5 Flat steel clamps 50/50/5 mm at both ends of each panel
6 Anchoring plate in the centre of the panel
7 Steel bar anchor 16 mm dia, 8 to every panel
8 Concrete component
9 White ceramic sheets 6/25 cm

The tower is a reinforced concrete structure. The external walls are of cavity construction. The outer skin is a storey height cladding panel, which were made complete with their ceramic cladding on a vibratory table as a precast unit, with an insulating panel stuck to the inside face. These units were erected with a tower crane and served as permanent shuttering for the insitu concrete. In order to drain away any condensation, a lead pipe of 8 mm dia was built into the horizontal joint of every element.

1 : 50

University Centre, University of Cambridge, England
Architects: Howell, Killick, Partridge and Amis, London

The building is clad with slabs of pink/grey limestone 4 cm
thick, secured with rust free hexagonal steel screws. Air
space behind the panels is 6 cm. All flashings in the window
areas are of lead sheet

Natural stone panels

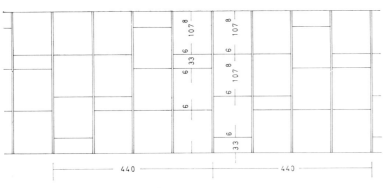

1:100

Museum in The Hague, Holland
Designed by the Municipal Building Department of The Hague
Manufacturer of the natural stone Travertine slabs: Albert Burrer, Maulbronn, West Germany
Contractors: Messrs van Stokkum, NV, Venlo, Holland

1 Gauinger Travertine roughly polished, 40 mm thick. Slab width approx 110 cm, 107.8 and 33 cm high
2 Stainless steel anchor
3 Air space 25 mm
4 Brickwork
5 Steel columns
6 Aluminium foil
7 Chipboard
8 Convector heater

1:10

Top lighted museum, Stuttgart
Architect: Günter Wilhelm and Jürgen Schwarz, Stuttgart

Wall cladding of conglomerate shell concrete, 40 mm thick. The slabs are 42, 72, and 120 cm wide and 35 to 180 cm high. Joint widths 14 mm and 40 mm. Expansion joints every 6.5 m, 40 mm wide. The slabs are fixed with galvanised anchors in the bed joints.

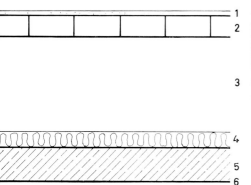

1 : 20

1 Plaster 2 cm
2 Free standing exhibition wall of 11.5 cm brickwork
3 Airspace 50 cm with room connection
4 Insulation 8 cm
5 Concrete 18 cm
6 Air space 3 cm
7 Natural stone slabs 4 cm

Thermopane glass

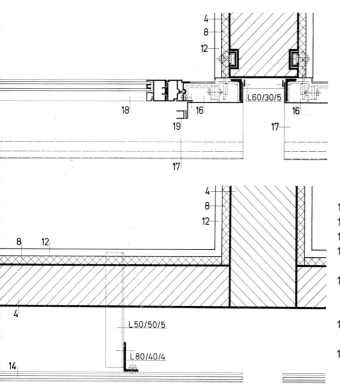

1 Concrete roof
2 Precast concrete column
3 Precast concrete flower box
4 Pumice wall
5 Polystyrene board
6 Steel frames of 'U' section sprayed asbestos
7 Cork
8 Mineral wool sheet
9 Coco matting
10 Screed
11 Floor covering
12 Plaster
13 'L' section steel fire protected
14 Thermopane glass, white, 62/144 cm, 6 mm thick
15 Roller blind box of sheet steel
16 Sprayed asbestos steel sheet window head

17 Window sill
18 Light metal pivot hung window
19 Light metal roller blind rail
20 Plastic roller blind
21 Radiator

University of Heidelberg, Germany: Nurses and staff building
Architect: Lothar Götz, Heidelberg

The 11 storey building belongs to the new clinic area of the University of Heidelberg. The windowless walls are constructed in exposed concrete. Window aprons are clad with white Thermopane glass sheets. Exposed steel components are fire protected. Window frames are aluminium.

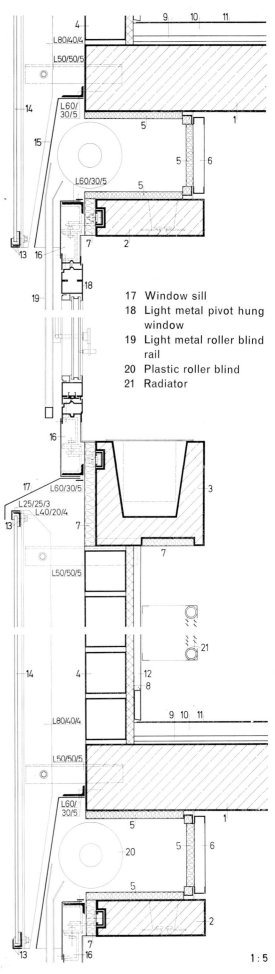

1 : 5

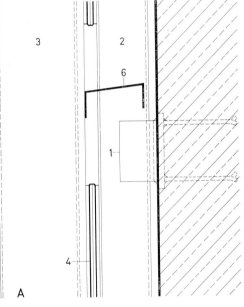

Store and restaurant in Munich
Architect: Rudolph Schütze, Munich. Architect for the facade: Franz Hart, Munich. Glass manufacturer: Schöninger Werkstätten oHG, Munich

12-storey tower block with curtain wall of grey Sekurit-glass. To the left and right of the tower two 4-storey buildings with movable aluminium louvres forming the elevations.

1 U 50/50/4 mm, 80 mm high, anchored to steel plates set in the concrete wall
2 Square steel section 100/40/3 mm   3 Aluminium mullion
4 Pretensioned cast glass, grey, 6 mm thick, pane size 178/159 cm
5 Aluminium mounting always in the centre of the glass pane, to take wind pressure (German patent: Messrs Schöninger)
6 Aluminium window sill to throw off driving rain and to break up ascending warm air currents
7 Connector at the abutment between the mullions

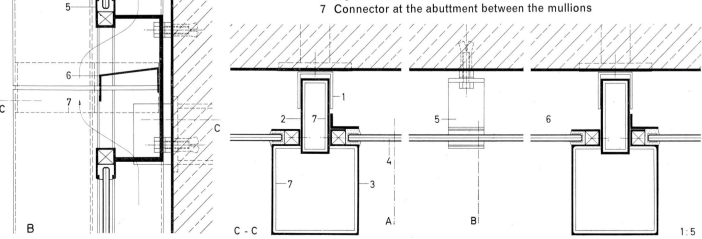

1:5

Glass sheets

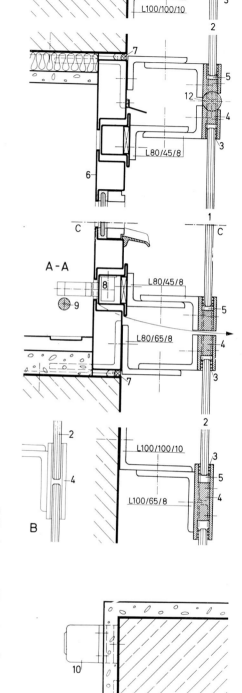

Municipal Theatre in Bonn
Architects: Klaus Gessler and Wilfred Beck-Erlang, Stuttgart
Manufacturers of the glass facade: Hermann Rüter-Stahlbau, Langenhagen, Hann

The wall behind the glass is painted grey/black, so that it recedes optically and the glass retains some of its green lustre. The fly tower is expressed with a surface of pleated concrete. Stage tower and auditorium are clad with silver anodised aluminium coffering.

1 Pretensioned crystal mirror glass 10-12 mm mounted on the movable window sashes, approx 2.10/1.10 m
2 Reeded mirror glass pretensioned, 10-12 mm, fixed in front of the wall surface, approx 2.10/1 m to 2.10/1.80 m
3 Chipboard
4 Bronze clamp, external cover plate screwed on
5 Plastic plug
6 Steel sheet 2 mm fire protected
7 Durable mastic
8 Flush bolt housing
9 Transverse shaft for the hinged casement opener
10 Mechanism for hinged sash opener
11 Steel sheet 1.5 mm, fire protected
12 Pivot of the hinged sash
13 Hinge for access for cleaning

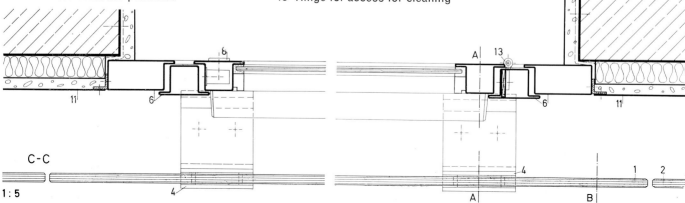

C-C

1 : 5

Vita Life Assurance, Stuttgart
Architect: Wilfried Beck-Erlang, Stuttgart

A basic condition in the design of this facade was that the offices behind the facade should be protected from the street noise. This was achieved with a glass sheet screen of 12 mm thickness which, by means of its weight and the various inclinations, reduces the sound correspondingly. The office windows behind can be opened and consist of aluminium frames with Thermopane glass.

1 Steel sheet 2 mm
2 Glass clamp of chrome nickel steel
3 Durable mastic
4 Pretensioned crystal mirror glass 12 mm, maximum size 180/199 cm
5 Pretensioned cast glass 12 mm
6 Mobile ladder for facade cleaning, in storage position in the photo
7 Spurs 8 cm dia, all 28 cm

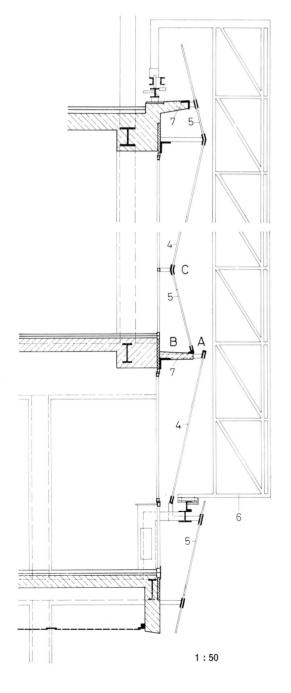

1 : 50

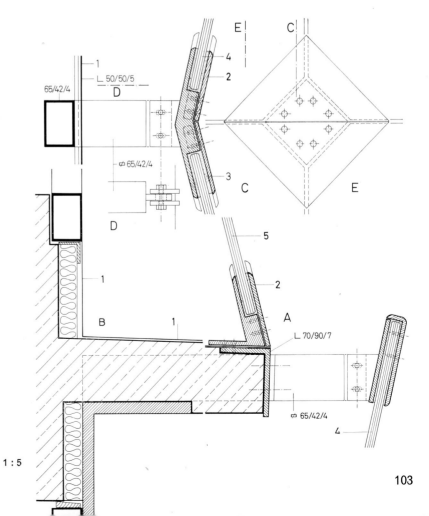

1 : 5

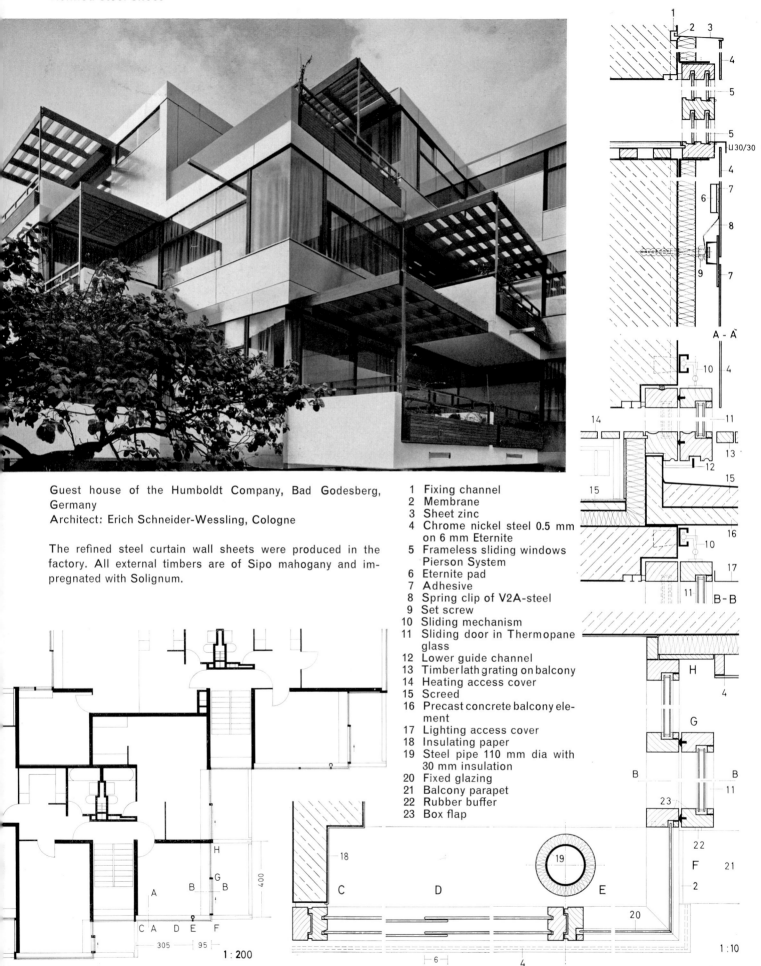

Guest house of the Humboldt Company, Bad Godesberg, Germany
Architect: Erich Schneider-Wessling, Cologne

The refined steel curtain wall sheets were produced in the factory. All external timbers are of Sipo mahogany and impregnated with Solignum.

1 Fixing channel
2 Membrane
3 Sheet zinc
4 Chrome nickel steel 0.5 mm on 6 mm Eternite
5 Frameless sliding windows Pierson System
6 Eternite pad
7 Adhesive
8 Spring clip of V2A-steel
9 Set screw
10 Sliding mechanism
11 Sliding door in Thermopane glass
12 Lower guide channel
13 Timber lath grating on balcony
14 Heating access cover
15 Screed
16 Precast concrete balcony element
17 Lighting access cover
18 Insulating paper
19 Steel pipe 110 mm dia with 30 mm insulation
20 Fixed glazing
21 Balcony parapet
22 Rubber buffer
23 Box flap

Refectory for the University of Edinburgh, Scotland
Architects: Rowand, Anderson, Kininmonth and Paul,
Edinburgh

The building is of steel skeleton construction. The walls are fully
glazed in the ground storey. The upper storey is clad 3.30 m
high in lead sheet, laid on 30 mm diagonal softwood boarding
covered with Kraft paper. The sheets are 2 mm thick, 60 cm wide
and up to 215 cm high. The lateral abutments of the sheets are
in the height of the building.
In the assembly a strip of copper sheet 5 cm wide was fixed to
the wall at every 60 cm, under all vertical joints and was bent
twice into the lead seam. In the horizontal overlapping of the
lead, the upper sheet was fixed with two strips of lead bent up
over the lower edge. The lead cladding is dressed over the roof
edge to form a flashing.
The upper storey has no windows, only four openings for the
ventilation. Frames and sills are lead covered.

Enamelled sheets

Offices in Rheinhausen, Germany
Design: Friedrich Krupp Bauplanung,
Essen

The building is 64 m long and 48 m wide.
Column grid 8 mm, 5 storey steel construction. Construction assembly method
developed by Krupp. The floor to ceiling
windows have no apron or sill, and are
mounted between the edge beams of the
floor slabs.

1 Steel sheet white enamelled on bearing plates
2 Continuous steel angles 80/60/6 mm
3 Stop angle welded to the edge bearer
4 Welded sheet steel box profile columns
5 Edge bearer of 10 mm sheet steel, with
welded projecting angles above and
below
6 Cork granule sheet 4 cm
7 Fixed glazed window in steel frame
8 Gutter
9 Heat insulation, also serving as fire
resistance
10 Steel sheet beam
11 Suspended ceiling
12 Steel segment ceiling of 2 mm steel
sheet
13 Oppanol
14 Precast concrete slabs
15 Screed
16 Ventilation apparatus

A Vertical section
B Horizontal section

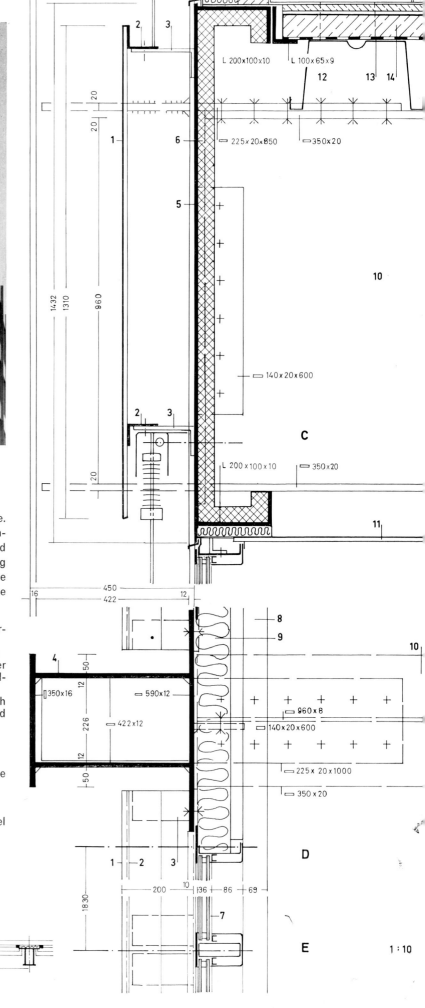

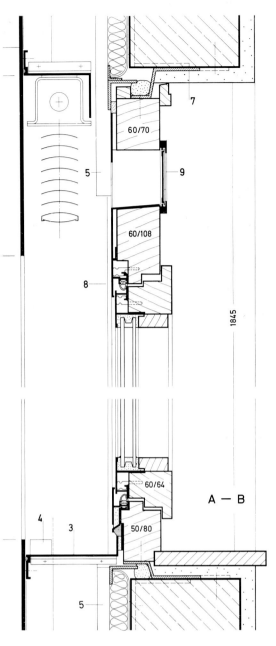

Office block for Siemens AG, Düsseldorf
Planning and project management by
Siemens Building Department
Direction: Willy Thormann, Erlangen
Development and installation of facade:
Messrs Ritter Aluminium GmbH, Köngen,
Neckar and Messrs Hermann Hassler KG
(window and door factory), Würges, Taunus

1 Natural anodised aluminium element 175 cm wide, 375 cm high, 5 mm thick
2 Box profile for support
3 Window sill sloping to the outside
4 Rain water outlet in the box section, thus avoiding staining on the front elevation
5 Slit for permanent ventilation
6 Base construction galvanised; fixing on NP 8 with 3 adjustable connectors every storey height
7 Window surround
8 Timber/aluminium window with side hung sash
9 Permanent ventilation

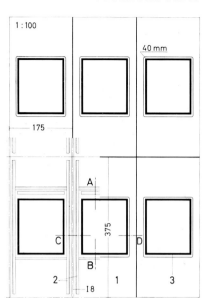

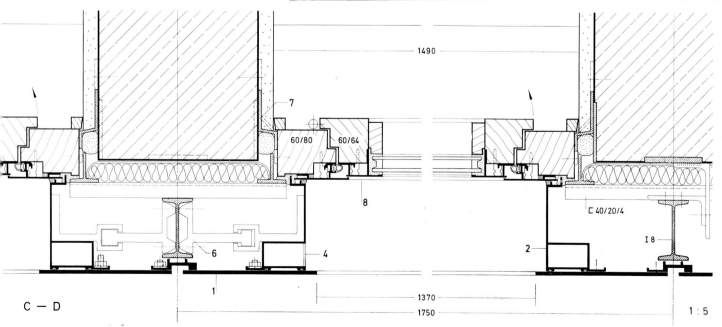

C — D

1 : 5

Cast aluminium sheets

Office and business premises in Stuttgart
Architect: Paul Stohrer, Stuttgart

Manufacturer of the aluminium sheets: Wutöschingen
Aluminium Works GmbH, Wutöschingen

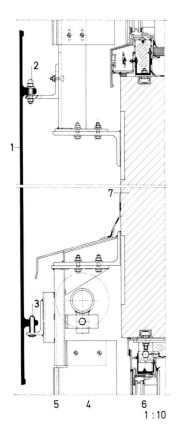

1 Aluminium cast sheet with four cast on lugs. Sheet thickness approx 15 mm; continuous edge strengthening, approx 15 mm
2 Vertical screws of stainless steel set on plastic washers
3 Plastic covered locking pin
4 Aluminium sheet blind
5 Guide of the roller blind housing
6 Aluminium fixed window anodised dark grey, glazed with Thermopane glass
7 Window apron in reinforced concrete. All supports in the base construction are galvanised steel sections

1 Element frames of aluminium sections, externally anodised grey (Grinatal), naturally anodised internally. Insulated with synthetic rubber Kautschuk

2 Joining glass, in every case fixed glazed above with a hung casement below

3 Columns covered with grey aluminium (Grinatal-section)

4 Sandwich sheet covered both sides with aluminium

5 Aluminium cast sheet GAR 12 Si open oven poured

6 Roller blind housing

7 Aluminium sheet

8 Galvanised sheet steel

9 Insulation – polyurethane foam

10 1/2 INP 34

11 Sprayed asbestos as fire protection

Offices of the Winterthur Life Assurance, Winterthur, Switzerland
Architect: E. Bosshardt, Winterthur

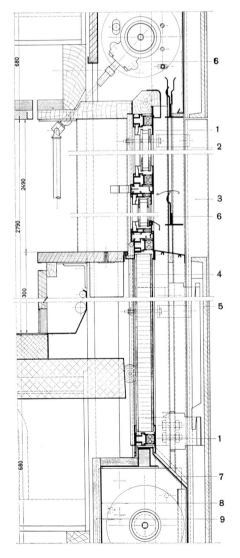

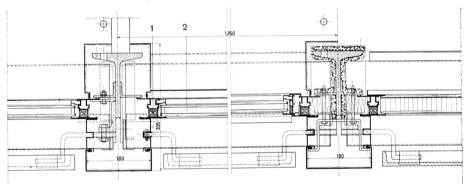

1 : 10

Cast aluminium sheets

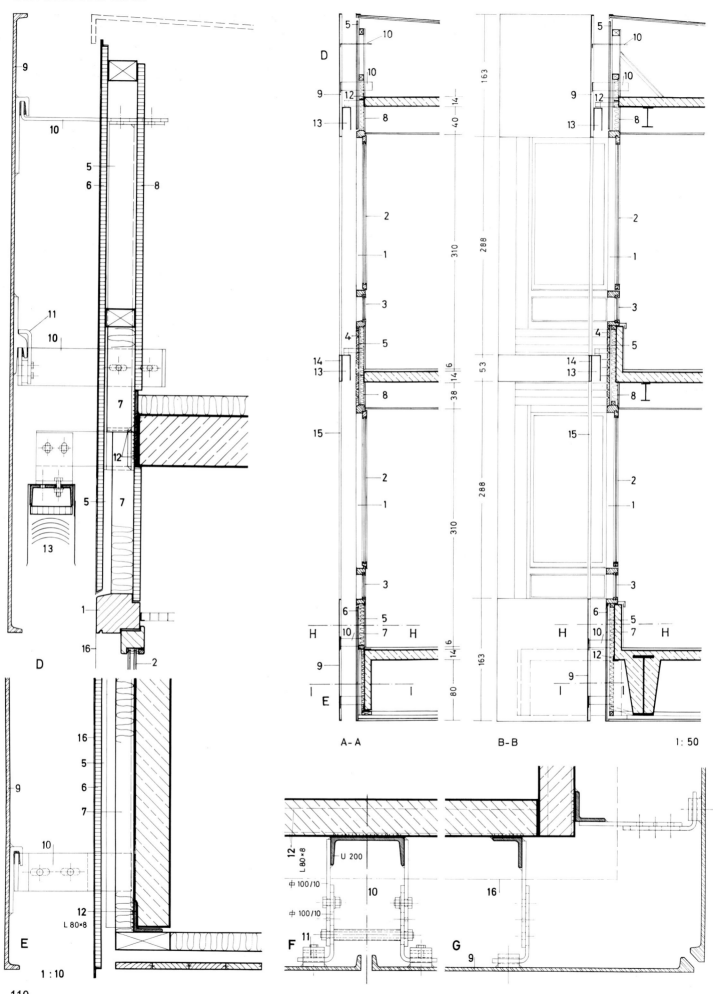

A-A

B-B

1 : 50

E   1 : 10

F   G

Council building of the Federal Constitutional Tribunal in Karlsruhe, Germany: Judges' building
Contractor: The German Federal Republic
Architect: Paul Baumgarten, Berlin, in collaboration with Berndt Zachariae
Project management: Municipal Construction Board II, Karlsruhe

1 Curtain wall framed construction in Oregon pine
2 Double pane safety glass. The windows are partially fixed glazed, or installed as sliding or pivot hung sashes
3 Hung casement
4 Oregon pine boarding 3/10 cm
5 Air space
6 Chipboard sheet 19 mm, covered with 1 mm standing seam aluminium roof sheeting, untreated
7 Insulation
8 Chipboard 19 mm
9 Cast aluminium sheets (open oven poured with optional exposed surface) average thickness 12 mm
10 Edge strengthening and diagonal stiffening ribs 40 mm thick. Every sheet has four cleats welded on for fixing
11 Locking device 1 per sheet

12 Continuous steel profiles anchored in the concrete as base construction for the vertical 'L' and corresponding 'T' steels on which the clamps (see 10) are fixed.
Crosspiece cut away in the area of the perpendicular section
13 Roller blinds automatically controlled, but each individually regulated
14 Removable cover of anodised aluminium sheet
15 Connecting tubes, natural anodised aluminium
16 Outer edge of the external skin

A-A and B-B: Vertical sections of the first and second upper storeys

On account of the surrounding parks only single rooms are air conditioned; windows in others open. In order to keep down heat loss through walls and windows, electrically controlled blinds are placed outside the windows as shutters. Cast aluminium sheets placed in front of the wall surfaces act as reflectors, whose apron elements are themselves also rear ventilated.

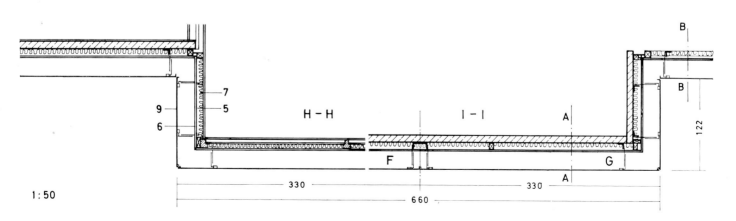

1:50

Cast aluminium element

BMW offices, Munich
Architect: Dr Karl Schwanzer, Vienna
Installation of the facade: Götz Metal Construction, Munich

1 Guide strip
2 Neoprene section
3 Thread housing ready cast
4 Clamp for the facade element
5 Steel angle for fixing the guide channel
6 Alcast facade element (see also the text on opposite page)
7 Heat insulation 3 and 5 cm thick
8 Window of two pane insulation glass inclined at the top about 9° towards the outside
9 Aluminium window frames
10 Aluminium fixed bead
11 Aluminium sheet cladding
12 Concrete column in every sixth axis
13 Insulation panel 6 cm thick
14 Mineral wool

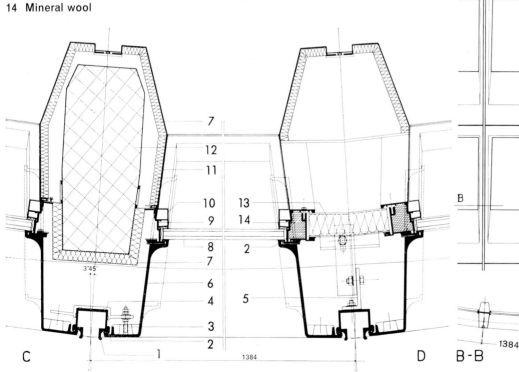

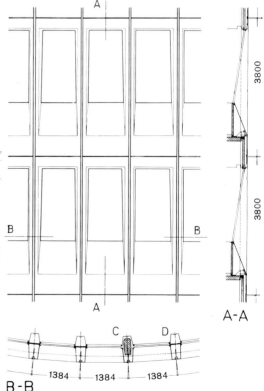

◁

Opposite:
For the facade elements of the BMW administration building cast aluminium panels of storey height were manufactured and mounted as a cold facade, with rear ventilation. The size of one element 138/382 cm. Fixing of the massive skin is by a hinge-type cramp and laterally with aluminium 'U' channel sections (see 1 on diagram opposite). The horizontal junction of the elements is formed as a free encroachment (rear ventilated). Here also the resulting movements due to temperature and structural variations are contained within each storey. The inner insulating wall and the windows are fixed after the element is assembled. The storeys were enclosed in the erection process, every completed storey being fitted immediately with the cladding elements, including insulation and window. For this reason the internal construction and finishing could commence during the rough carcassing.
Licence holder for Alcast Elements in Europe is Swiss Aluminium AG, Zürich.

Above:
Offices of the Life Insurance Co, Chiyoda Seimei, Tokyo
Architects: Tohgo Murano and Mori, Tokyo

Curtain facade of aluminium, approx 1.6 m in front of the window wall and fixed to the projecting floor slabs. The elements were poured in sand moulds. Wall thicknesses 6-8 mm. Each unit is asembled out of four parts: the outer and inner skins for the support and the two sill areas. The screwed joint is in the vertical groove, as clearly seen in the photograph. Between the elements are expansion joints of 12 mm sealed with Thiokol.
These thin wall, three dimensional Alcast-elements can be produced today in sizes up to 4 m high and 1.8 m wide. Stiffening ribs, fixing points, among other things, can be cast in with the panel, the panels being delivered ready for mounting.

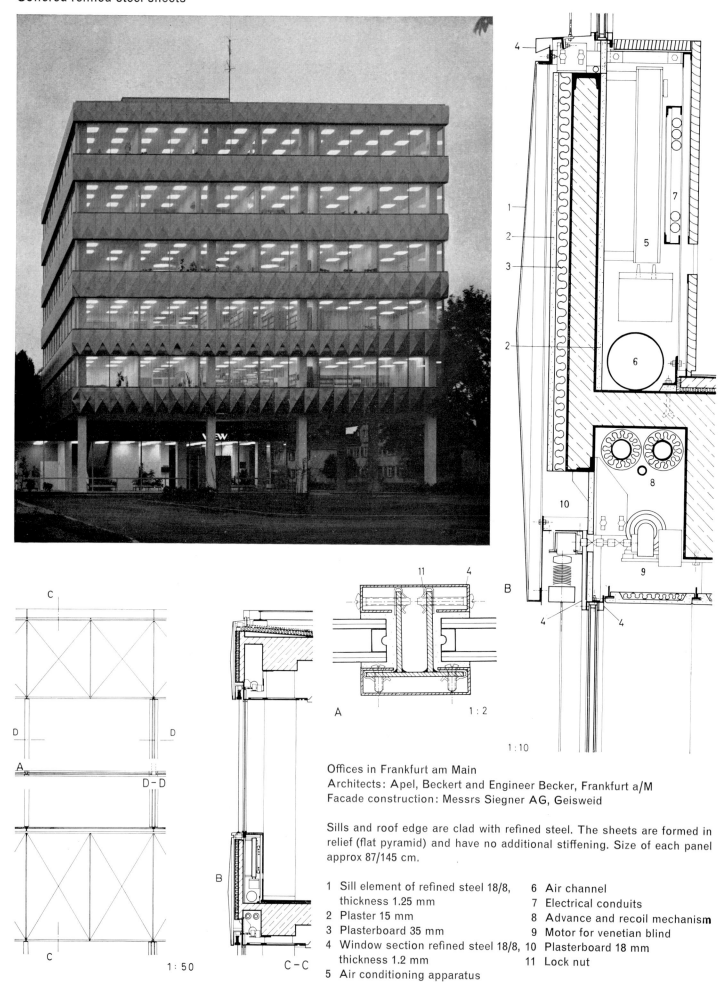

Offices in Frankfurt am Main
Architects: Apel, Beckert and Engineer Becker, Frankfurt a/M
Facade construction: Messrs Siegner AG, Geisweid

Sills and roof edge are clad with refined steel. The sheets are formed in relief (flat pyramid) and have no additional stiffening. Size of each panel approx 87/145 cm.

1 Sill element of refined steel 18/8, thickness 1.25 mm
2 Plaster 15 mm
3 Plasterboard 35 mm
4 Window section refined steel 18/8, thickness 1.2 mm
5 Air conditioning apparatus
6 Air channel
7 Electrical conduits
8 Advance and recoil mechanism
9 Motor for venetian blind
10 Plasterboard 18 mm
11 Lock nut

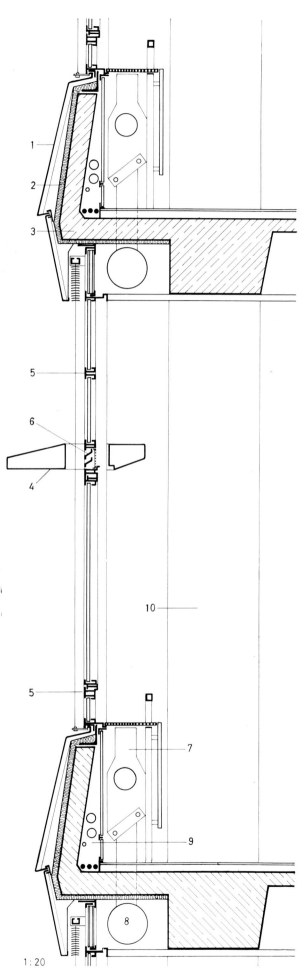

1 : 20

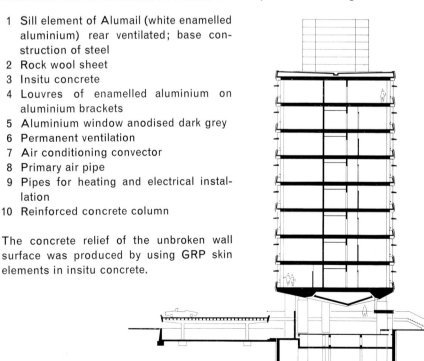

IBM offices, Berlin
Architects: Rolf Gutbrod and Dr Bernhard Binder, Berlin and Stuttgart

1 Sill element of Alumail (white enamelled aluminium) rear ventilated; base construction of steel
2 Rock wool sheet
3 Insitu concrete
4 Louvres of enamelled aluminium on aluminium brackets
5 Aluminium window anodised dark grey
6 Permanent ventilation
7 Air conditioning convector
8 Primary air pipe
9 Pipes for heating and electrical installation
10 Reinforced concrete column

The concrete relief of the unbroken wall surface was produced by using GRP skin elements in insitu concrete.

1 : 500

115

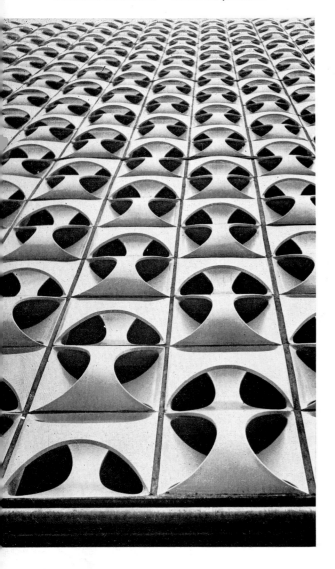

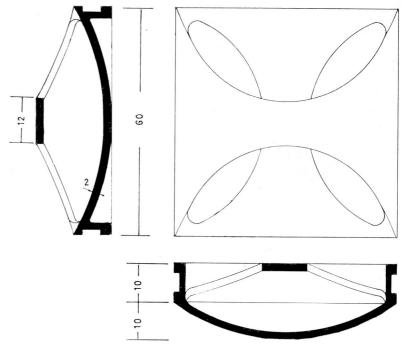

Merkur Store, Stuttgart
Architect: Dr Inge E. h. Egon Eiermann
Manufacturer of the ceramic components: Elemental-Baukeramik-Vertriebs GmbH, Ratingen

Merkur in Stuttgart was the first store to have a curtain wall of ceramic components. Planning began in 1957, and the building was completed at the end of 1960. In the design of the external wall the architect was obliged to conform to certain basic conditions:
(1) In every storey external galleries were required as escape ways in case of fire, and for the use of the fire brigade
(2) These galleries were not to be visible
(3) Windows and enclosing wall component were to be removable at all times.
The cladding elements weigh 95 kp/m²

Sprung rib sheet made of Hostalit Z
Manufacturer: Schildkröt Plastic Works AG, Mannheim

Rigid PVC sheets delivery size 93/345 cm. Profile height 17 mm. Weight 2.5 kp/². The material can be cut. Cover section for edges, corners and base are delivered in the same material. The sheets can be fixed to flat wall surfaces without any base construction. The rear ventilation is guaranteed by the wave form development of the ribs. The section drawn below is through the rib. The horizontal and vertical section can be considered identical. Besides the small chequered surfaces illustrated, other patterns are available in white or light grey.
According to the manufacturers only the first sheet need be plumbed in the assembly of the facade, since successive sheets will be correspondingly perpendicular. Drilling is done through the plate directly into the wall. The dowels (Fischer dowels) are brought together with about two turns of a screw. The screw is then tightened. Distance between fixing points horizontally and vertically is 45 cm.

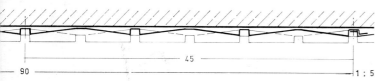

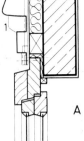

Flats and store, 'Alter Fritz', Berlin
Architects: Hans C. Müller and Georg Heinrichs, Berlin

1 Moulded sheets of Hostalit Z
2 Strawboard sheets and softwood battens as permanent shuttering
3 Reinforced concrete
4 Plastic coated sheets as permanent shuttering
5 Double glazed window
6 Chromed nickel steel screws
7 Plastic cap, periodically at the point of intersection of the sheet joints
8 Strips of plastic for receiving the vertical sheet joints

The building 'Alter Fritz' was one of the first with a facade cladding of plastic. The sheets are 70 cm high and up to 280 cm long. For the corners of the building angle pieces were welded together. On the long sides of the sheets are horizontal slots, approx every 70 cm corresponding to the position of the vertical battens (see 2). The assembly proceeds from top to bottom. The visible fixings in the photograph below are only temporary pins. In each case the upper edge of a sheet lies ready assembled under the adjoining sheet.

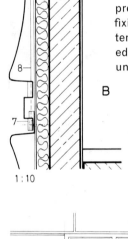

1:10

1:100

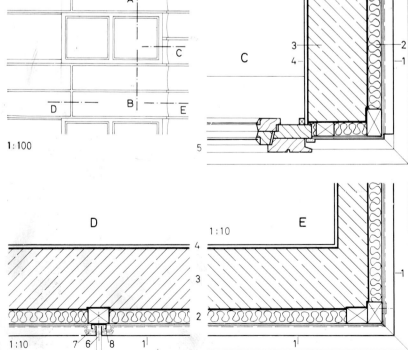

1:10

117

Coffered plastics

Technical University, Berlin: Institute for Technical Chemistry
Architect: Willi Kreuer, Berlin
Project management: Senator for Construction and Housing, Berlin

1 Trough element of Hostalit Z, 175 cm long, approx 95 cm high
2 Base construction U 50 approx 58 cm, 1.83 m long
3 Clamp section and cover strip, aluminium
4 Aluminium cover section
5 Fixed glazed panes and sliding window with aluminium frames
6 Insulation 35 mm
7 Reinforced concrete
8 Air conditioning duct
9 Black-out blind
10 Water tank (storage)
11 Measuring room
12 Laboratory
13 Vestibule

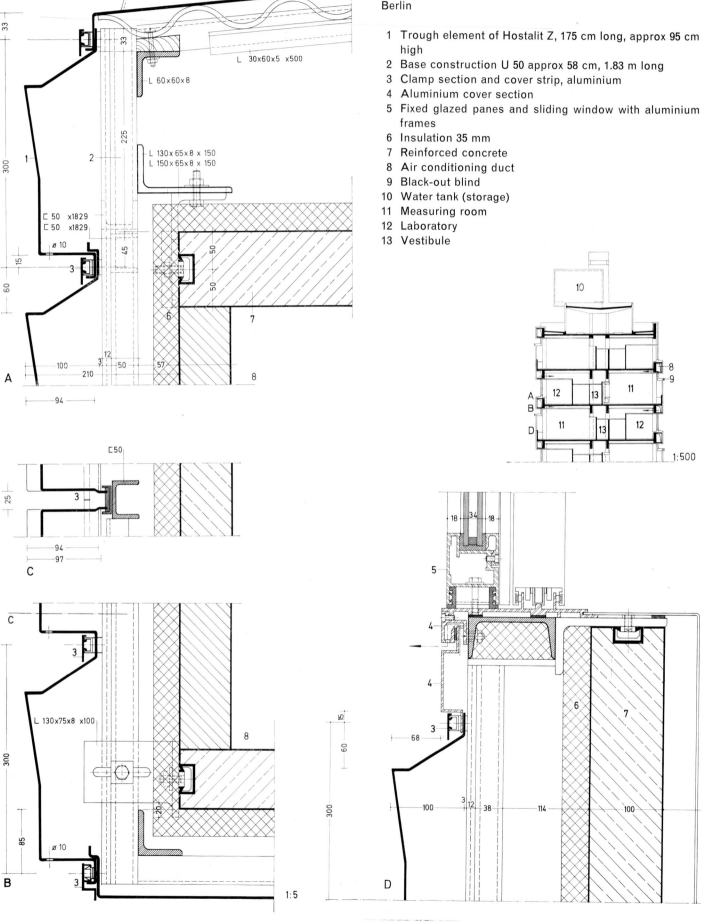

Technical University, Berlin: Institute for Technical Chemistry
Architect: Willi Kreuer, Berlin
Project management: Senator for Construction and Housing, Berlin

A conflagration test was carried out, in consideration of fire regulation requirements. Results: Hostalit Z did not drip or extend the fire and charred only in the area of the flames. At that time steel base construction was demanded. Today, however, the restrictions are easier and timber base construction is possible.†

County Court, Mannheim, Germany
Architect: Helmut Striffler, Mannheim-Lindenhof, in collabora-
tion with Lothar Otterbach, Horst Böhler, Edgar Vierneisel and
Heinz-Dieter Frank
Manufacturer of the facade cladding: Keller & Co GmbH,
Schifferstadt

Component parts of the cladding – sheets, sections, clamps,
screws and welding material – are of Cor-Ten steel.
In the screwed joints are separating washers of plastic to prevent
noise transmission. The back of the cladding panels are treated
with an anti-drumming material which neutralises the membrane
effect (oscillations) of the very thin sheets.

Opposite:
1 Dark grey anodised aluminium 2.5 mm
2 Electrically operated venetian blinds
3 Transome light fixed wired glass: fire stop
4 Aluminium sliding window glazed Thermopane glass
5 Eternit – Silan – sheet 57 mm thick
6 Air conditioning apparatus or convector
7 Service duct
8 Electrical conduits
9 Filing cabinet
10 Edge beam
11 Suspended metal ceiling
12 Screed

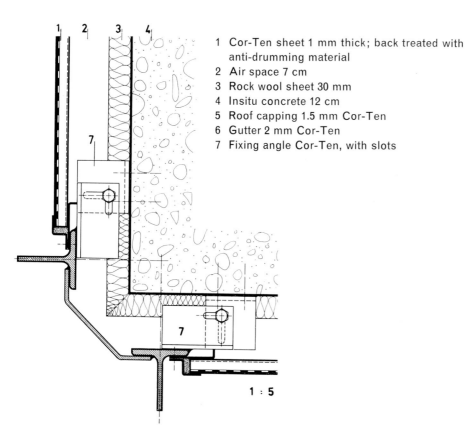

1 Cor-Ten sheet 1 mm thick; back treated with
  anti-drumming material
2 Air space 7 cm
3 Rock wool sheet 30 mm
4 Insitu concrete 12 cm
5 Roof capping 1.5 mm Cor-Ten
6 Gutter 2 mm Cor-Ten
7 Fixing angle Cor-Ten, with slots

1 : 5

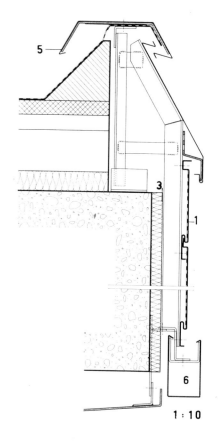

1 : 10

Judicial chancery, Heidelberg
Architect: Dieter A. Baumann, Karlsruhe, in collaboration with Freund, Ringe and Rosewich

The development consists of several buildings erected in the same style. Construction assembly system in composite precast reinforced concrete components with an aluminium curtain wall facade.

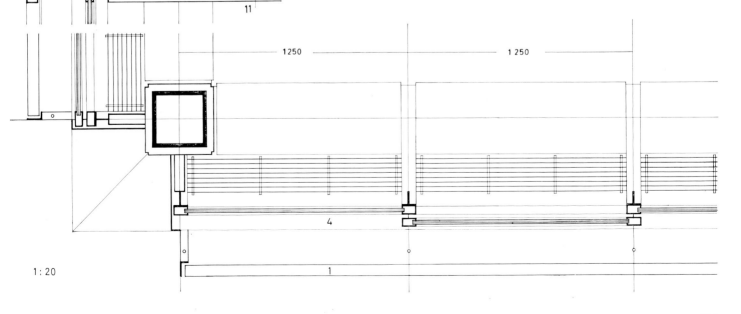

1 : 20

8

Sheet pile wall section – Cor-Ten steel

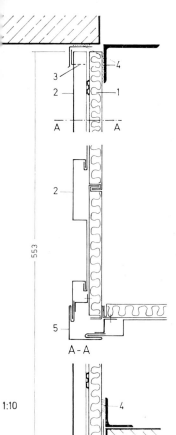

IBM Works, Austin, Texas, USA
Architects: Page, Southerland & Page
Wall cladding: R. C. Mahon Company, Warren, Michigan
Steel: Bethlehem Steel Corporation, Chesterton, Indiana

Sheet pile wall section: The sheets are fixed top and bottom with clip sections on horizontal assembly strips. There are insulation strips at points where various materials come together, as well as between metal and wall and between various different metals. The Mayari-R-Weathering steel, developed by the Bethlehem Steel Corporation and similar to Cor-Ten steel shown on page 120, forms a thick brown oxidised film on its surface preventing further deterioration.

1 Galvanised steel sheet 0.9 mm glued to 40 mm glass wool sheets
2 External cladding of weather resistant steel sheet 1.3 mm; cladding sheets, clamps strip and fixings are all of the same material
3 Angle piece: this is cut in the horizontal plane to fit the profile of the cladding sheets
4 Insulating strips
5 Removable corner section of galvanised steel sheet 1.3 mm, painted black
6 Lower sill covered with continuous aluminium sheet under the wall cladding and between the aluminium windows

Machine Factory Deckel, Munich
Architect: Dr Ing Walter Henn, Braunschweig

1 Zinc sheet
2 Flat steel plates, all 60 cm
3 Angle steel 20/20/3 mm
4 Flat steel 30/4 mm
5 Aluminium fascia sheet
6 Ytong block wall 12.5 cm
7 Timber batten 30/50 mm
8 Aluminium clip
9 Aluminium profile sheet
10 NPI 14
11 Clamp plate construction for
the Ytong blocks
12 Plasterboard 2.5 cm, skim
plaster 2 cm

A cladding with profiled sheets is very suitable for a windowless surface because the profiled sheets can be installed in very tall sections. Here, for example, in some places over two storeys high – ie, approx 6 m. Strip widths are approx 60 cm for 3 profiles. The sections clamped onto fixing strips are without visible screws. The vertical positions of the fixing strips are approx 50 cm.

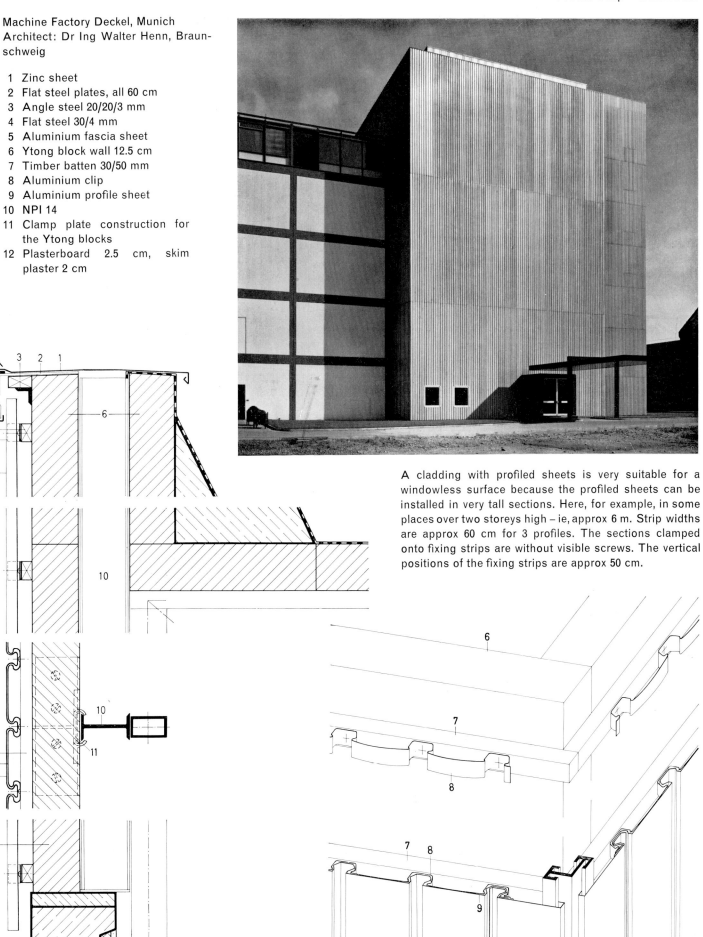

1:10

Profile strip – plastic

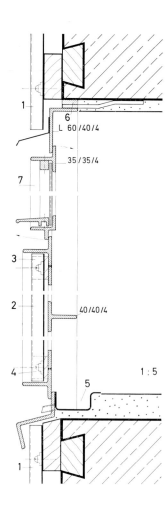

Multi-storey assembly building (above) and factory, Troisdorf, Germany
Design: Design Department of the Dynamit Nobel AG

1 Corrugated rigid PVC sheet – light grey
2 Corrugated rigid PVC sheet – transparent
3 Moulded timber fillet
4 Bronze screw with weather cap in every third corrugation trough
5 Condensation channel at floor level
6 Mastic sealing strip
7 Pivot hung window

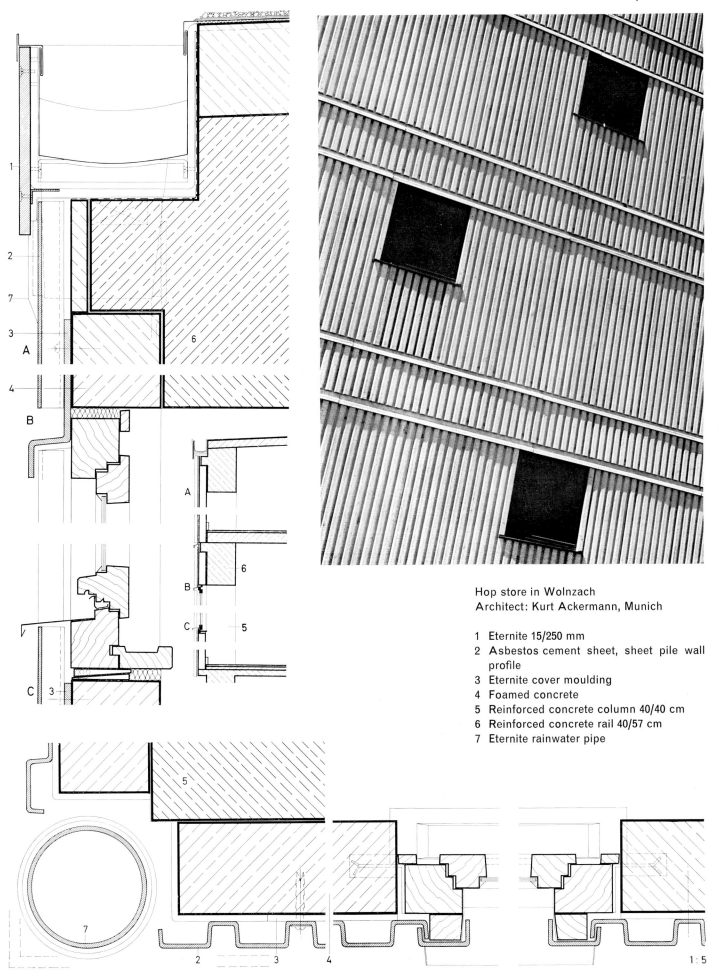

Hop store in Wolnzach
Architect: Kurt Ackermann, Munich

1 Eternite 15/250 mm
2 Asbestos cement sheet, sheet pile wall profile
3 Eternite cover moulding
4 Foamed concrete
5 Reinforced concrete column 40/40 cm
6 Reinforced concrete rail 40/57 cm
7 Eternite rainwater pipe

1 : 5

Curtain wall

Seagram Building, New York
Architect: Ludwig Mies van der Rohe

The facade of the Seagram Building, 1954-58, counts as the classic example of the curtain wall. Extruded sections of bronze (architectural bronze). The strong I-shaped mullions help to accentuate the verticals. Single glazed windows of room height with anti-glare glass, fixed glazed with screwed beading. Horizontal bands of sheet bronze without additional insulation, rear ventilated.

Lever Building, New York
Architects: Skidmore, Owings and Merrill, New York

The Lever Building, built in 1952, was the first building with a curtain wall. Mullion construction of steel sections, covered with stainless steel. Windows with heat absorbent glass, single glazed. The window aprons of wired cast glass are rear ventilated. Back-up walling is of foamed slag blocks, plastered. On the inside 5 cm glass wool as heat insulation.

Dominion Centre, Toronto, Canada
Design: Ludwig Mies van der Rohe
Architects: Sidney Bregman, Toronto, with
John B. Parkin Associates, and Bregman &
Hamann

The building group consists of a 56-storey
(left in the photograph) and a 46-storey
tower, with a 1-storey bank pavilion. Concrete
clad steel framing.
The columns lie behind the facade. Column
grid 30 × 40 feet: ie, 9.15 × 12.20 m.
Facade construction is of steel sections,
painted matt black, including the steel sheet
cover sections for the edges. The large
I-sections are connected every 2 storeys.
Storey height windows are glazed in brown/
grey heat absorbing glass, fixed glazed in
aluminium frames.

1 Permanent ventilation
2 Fixed glazing
3 Glass sheet grey/green 6 mm
4 Plasterboard sheet 8 mm
5 Glass wool 80 mm
6 All cover sections of chrome nickel steel
7 Asbestos
8 Veneered sheet
9 Vinyl sheet
10 Hard fibre sheet 4 mm
11 False base, 32 mm
12 High tension circuit channel
13 Socket outlet panel
14 Low tension circuit channel
15 Main mullion, 120/70 mm
16 Fixing of the main mullion

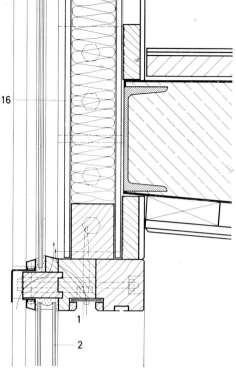

Jespersen office block, Copenhagen
Architect: Arne Jacobsen

Timber mullion construction clad with stainless steel, filled with glass.

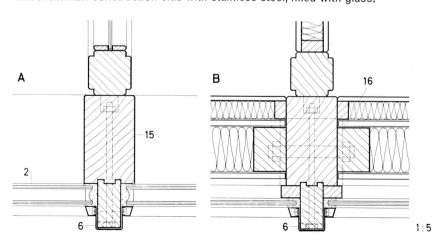

1 : 5

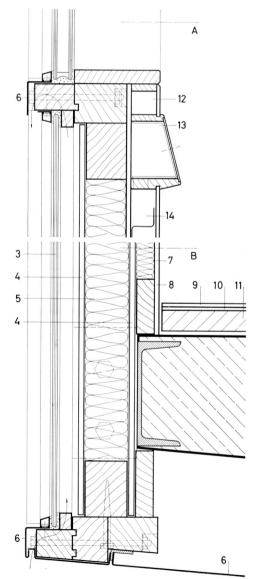

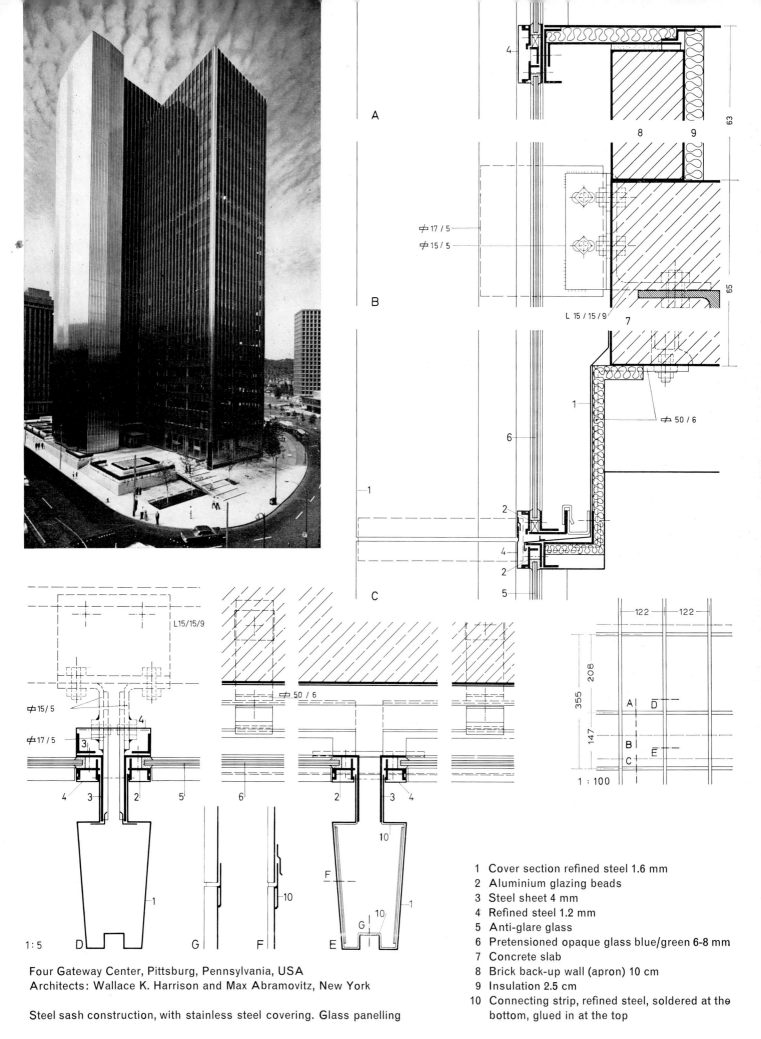

A

B

C

8   9

63

65

⌷ 17 / 5

⌷ 15 / 5

L 15 / 15 / 9

7

1

⌷ 50 / 6

6

2

4

2

5

1

L15/15/9

⌷ 15 / 5

⌷ 17 / 5

4

3

4   3   2   5

6   ⌷ 50 / 6   2   3   4

10

F

10

10

G

1:5   D   G   F   E

122   122

355   208   147

A   D

B   E

C

1 : 100

Four Gateway Center, Pittsburg, Pennsylvania, USA
Architects: Wallace K. Harrison and Max Abramovitz, New York

Steel sash construction, with stainless steel covering. Glass panelling

1 Cover section refined steel 1.6 mm
2 Aluminium glazing beads
3 Steel sheet 4 mm
4 Refined steel 1.2 mm
5 Anti-glare glass
6 Pretensioned opaque glass blue/green 6-8 mm
7 Concrete slab
8 Brick back-up wall (apron) 10 cm
9 Insulation 2.5 cm
10 Connecting strip, refined steel, soldered at the bottom, glued in at the top

129

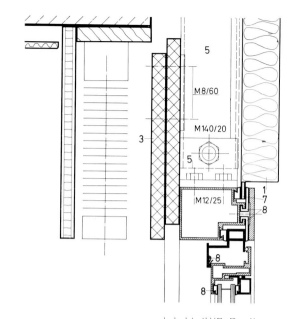

6 Refined steel sheets
7 Compressed cork
8 Neoprene
9 Pivot hung window 40 cm wide, to open 25 cm, glazed insulating glass. Lock in the fixed frame
10 Fixed glazing
11 Bore hole for the outlet of condensation
12 Rock wool
13 Butyl strip 2 mm
14 Gear for ventilation window

Dorland Advertising, Berlin
Architect: Rolf Gutbrod, Stuttgart and Berlin
Installation: Messrs Josef Gartner & Co, Gundelfingen

Mullion construction of aluminium, sill aprons of refined steel

1 Panel of refined steel with integral insulation lining
2 Aluminium section anodised, dark grey
3 Asbestolux sheet 400/20 mm
4 Hinged sash window with insulating glass
5 Square section steel pipe 80/40/4 mm

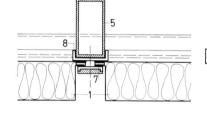

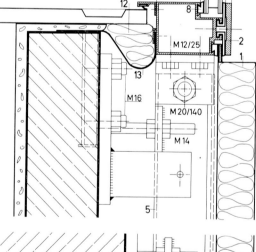

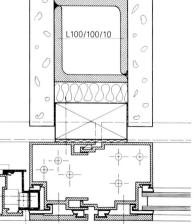

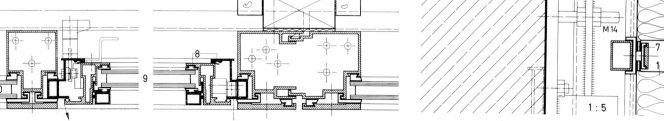

1 : 5

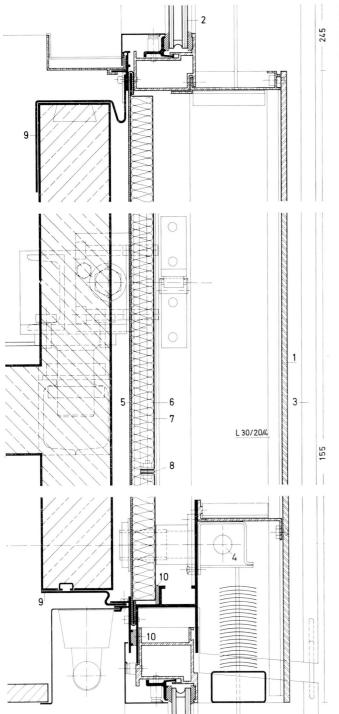

Osram offices, Munich
Architect: Dr Ing Walter Henn, Braunschweig
Installation: Messrs Josef Gartner & Co, Gundelfingen

Mullion construction and aluminium sill aprons

1:5

1 Aluminium 8 mm anodised
  light green
2 Insulation glass, fixed glazed
  in Neoprene sections
3 Aluminium sections
4 Spindle for blind
5 Butyl skin 2 mm
6 Foamed phenolic resin sheet
  30 mm
7 Galvanised steel sheet 1 mm
8 Butyl strip
9 Butyl sheet stuck to concrete
10 Neoprene

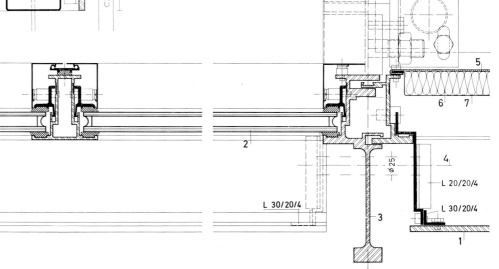

Curtain wall – panels

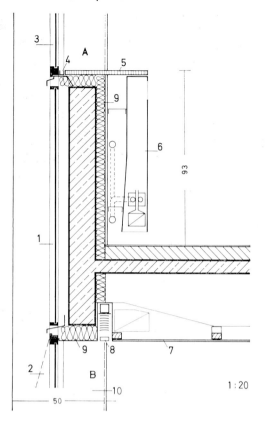

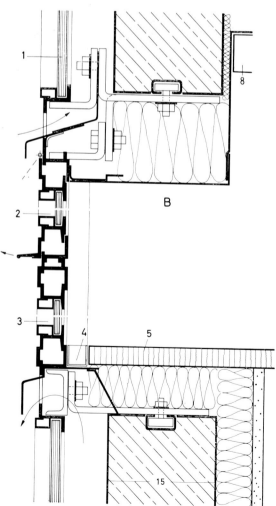

BAT House, Hamburg
Architects: Dr Ing Helmut Hentrich and Hubert Petschnigg, Düsseldorf

Concrete frame, built-in steel windows, sill aprons glass sheet panels

1 Apron cladding in Thermopane glass
2 Casement window mirror glass glazed 7-8 mm
3 Fixed window mirror glass glazed 7-8 mm
4 Condensation channel
5 Natural stone
6 Air conditioning apparatus
7 Plasterboard on battens 30/50 mm
8 Blind
9 Plasterboard
10 Reinforced concrete column clad externally with aluminium, heat insulated internally and plastered

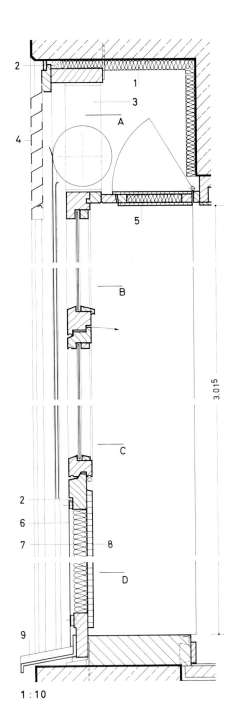

1 : 10

Higher Trade and Professional School, Heidelberg, Germany
Architect: Dr Ing Friedrich Wilhelm Kraemer, Braunschweig

Reinforced concrete frame with timber frames. Sill aprons enamelled steel
sheet

1 Plasterboard
2 Mastic sealer
3 Flat steel 100/5 mm as support for the roller blind
4 Air louvre of sheet steel 2 mm
5 Glass wool 25 mm between plywood sheets
6 White enamelled steel sheet
7 Rock wool 40 mm
8 Plywood 18 mm
9 Asbestos cement element
10 Centre mullion of double frame 10/4 with cover board 13/217 cm painted white
11 Sashes between the pivot windows

1 : 10

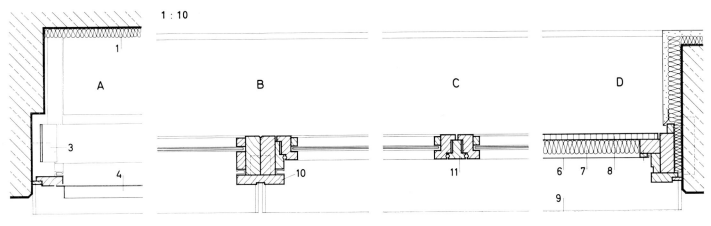

Curtain wall – mullions

Architect's office in Hagen, Germany
Architect: Hans Wenig, Hagen

Mullion construction of light steel sections clad with refined steel including the window aprons.

1 Roof parapet slates
2 Boarding
3 Stainless steel sheet 18/8, 1.25 mm thick
4 Mastic sealer
5 Packing piece
6 Sashes of galvanised and stove enamelled light steel sections covered with stainless steel sheet 18/8
7 Thermopane dry glazed into Neoprene special sections
8 Marble window sill
9 Butyl strip
10 18/8 sheet, 1.25 mm, chamfered, welded on the corners and stuck to the back panel
11 Compensating veneer stuck on to panel
12 Entrance door
13 18/8 clipped on section
14 Aluminium striking plate anthracite anodised

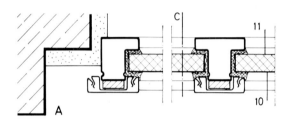

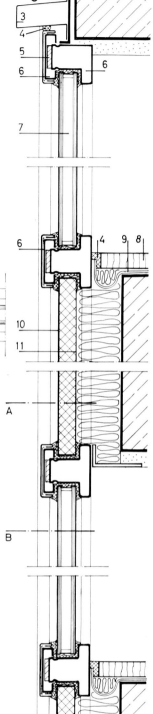

1 : 5

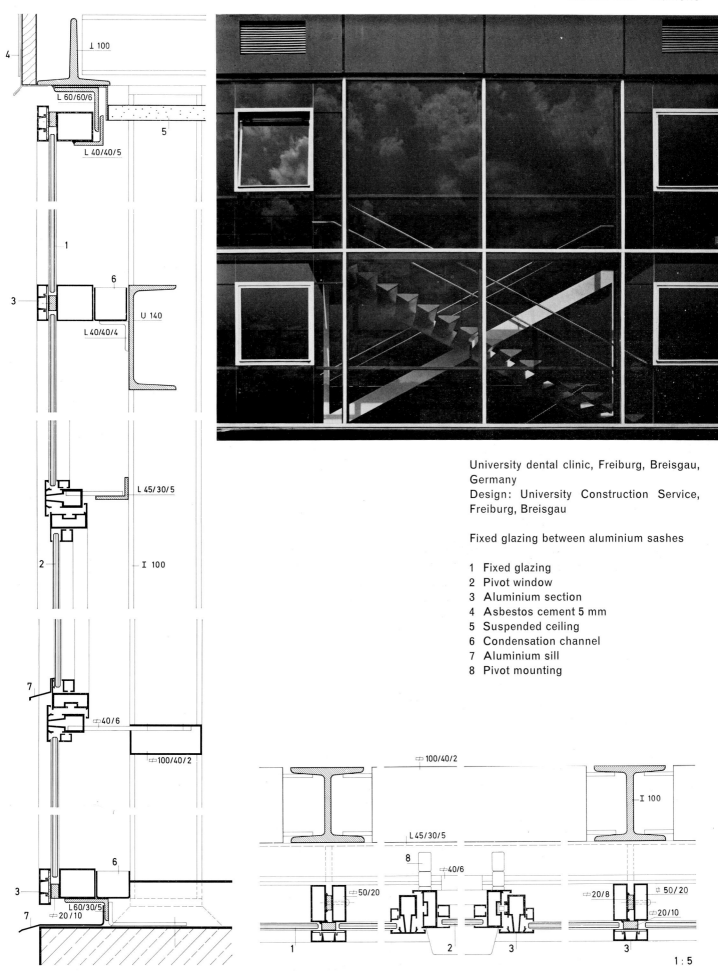

University dental clinic, Freiburg, Breisgau, Germany
Design: University Construction Service, Freiburg, Breisgau

Fixed glazing between aluminium sashes

1 Fixed glazing
2 Pivot window
3 Aluminium section
4 Asbestos cement 5 mm
5 Suspended ceiling
6 Condensation channel
7 Aluminium sill
8 Pivot mounting

1 : 5

135

Curtain wall – mullions

Only the horizontal bands are fixed. The parts in between can be exchanged if the function of a room needs to be altered. Their total height of 274 cm corresponds to the room height. The grid widths are 113 cm and 70 cm. Two-pane insulating glass is either fixed glazed or pivot hung windows. The narrow upper part of the windows are top hung.

The enclosing wall components consist of 80 mm thick plates (deep drawn) or as cantilevered projected cupboard elements with 40 mm thick walls. These boxes are 21 cm deep and 105 cm or 169 cm high. Wall construction: Cor-Ten steel sheet, stove enamelled internally, the intervening air space filled with polyurethane foam. The photographs show the facades before the completion of the patina formation, therefore the surfaces look patchy.

Free University, Berlin
Institute for German Philology and History
Architects: G. Candilis, A. Josic, S. Woods, M. Schiedhelm, Berlin;
Jean Prouvé, Paris, was associated with the design of the facade

Interchangeable facade elements of Cor-Ten steel

Office building in Stuttgart
Architect: Reiner R. Czermak, Stuttgart
Manufacturer of the facade elements: Neuffer Bros, Window Factory, Stuttgart

Timber curtain wall. Window aprons in enamelled sheet steel.

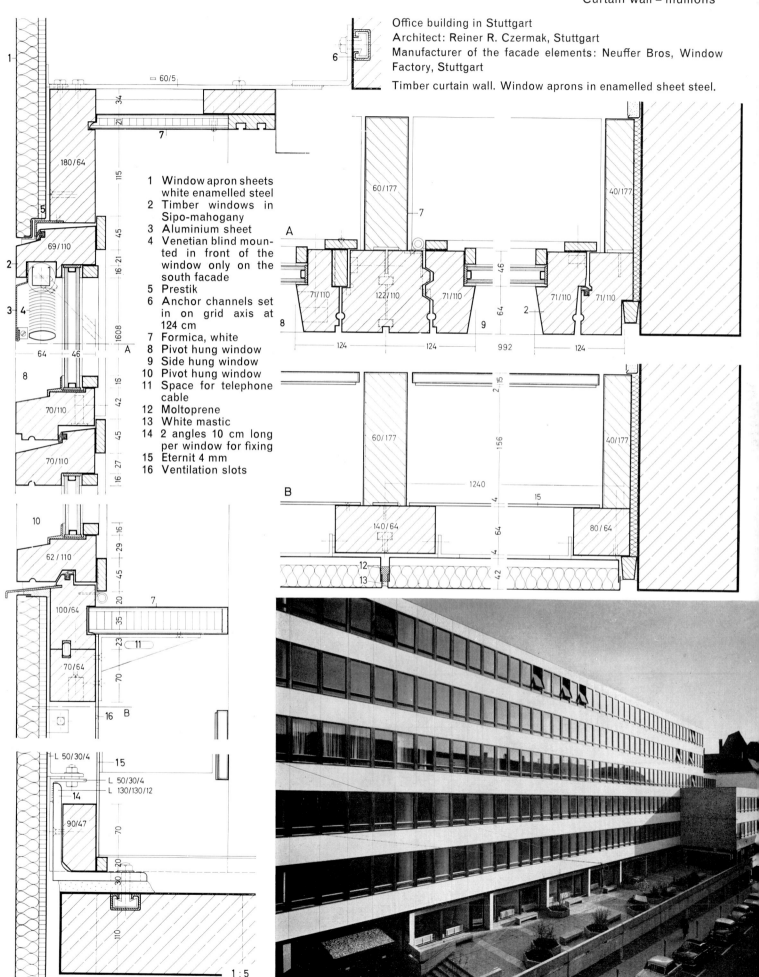

1 Window apron sheets white enamelled steel
2 Timber windows in Sipo-mahogany
3 Aluminium sheet
4 Venetian blind mounted in front of the window only on the south facade
5 Prestik
6 Anchor channels set in on grid axis at 124 cm
7 Formica, white
8 Pivot hung window
9 Side hung window
10 Pivot hung window
11 Space for telephone cable
12 Moltoprene
13 White mastic
14 2 angles 10 cm long per window for fixing
15 Eternit 4 mm
16 Ventilation slots

1 : 5

Curtain wall – mullions

Commercial Bank, Bielefeld, Germany
Architects: Dr Ing E. h. Heinrich Rosskotten, Edgar Tritthart
and Joachim Schiel, in collaboration with D. Ryang and W.
Mimm, Düsseldorf

Curtain walls are of teak. The factory-made frames were treated
with a non-film forming, pressure-impregnated wood preservative. The windows of room height are pivoted but they are only
opened for cleaning. In front of the slab edge and the air conditioning ducts in the floor space are plywood sandwich panels
with a core of glass wool. They are dipped in resin lacquer and
the joints are sealed with durable mastic. Their role in the
facade is emphasised by the strong profiles of the projecting
blind boxes

Commercial Bank, Bielefeld, Germany
Architects: Dr Ing E. h. Heinrich Rosskotten, Edgar Tritthart and Joachim Schiel, in collaboration with D. Ryang and W. Mimm, Düsseldorf

(a) Casement windows, teak frames; panes 11 mm plate glass
(b) Sandwich panels 6 mm
(c) Boxes of 2 mm copper sheet, 81 cm high, 15 cm deep, stiffened with fibreglass sheet stuck on the inside; the blinds are in the bottom
(d) Side enclosures of the boxes (c) of 2 mm copper sheet, at the free standing end covered by the bearing plate
(e) Struts of square-section copper tube 80/30 mm screwed to the mullions of the curtain wall with stainless steel screws
(f) Copper U-section with integral plastic lining as a guide for the blind
(g) Connecting bolts M 10 of solid copper with 50 mm dia copper nuts. At the connection points are plastic washers, which take up movement and avoid noise transmission

Curtain wall – light slabs

Commercial Bank, Düsseldorf
Architect: Paul Schneider-Esleben, Düsseldorf, in collaboration with Jürgen Ringel and Dieter Hoor

Reinforced concrete frame with aluminium curtain wall facade. Curtain wall element construction inspired by coach building techniques. Rounded corners without frames. The panels are framed out of deep drawn sheets. The units are comprised of three parts (panel, window, cover strip for horizontal points). They were delivered ready for assembly and erected from the cleaning cradle without scaffolding.

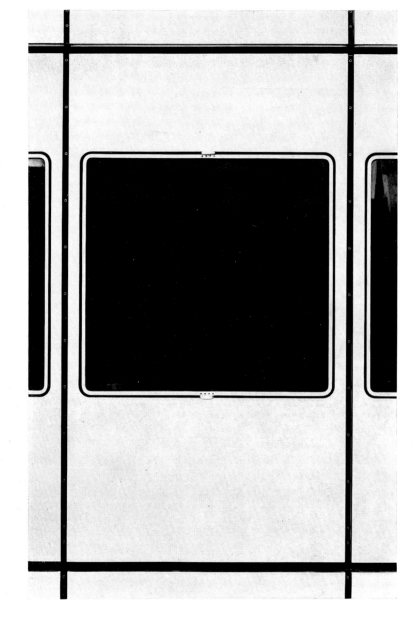

1 Storey height facade elements 172/310 cm, both sides of aluminium sheet 2 mm thick, anodised matt finish. Insulation: Air-Comb-Waben (Douglas-Air-Craft Corp, Santa Monica, USA)
2 Horizontal points, 6 cm wide (expansion points), membrane of pressed-on Neoprene section against the screwed-on cover strip of the upper element
3 Vertical points 3.5 cm wide. Neoprene-sheathed cover brads fixed with chromium steel screws (Imbus-screws)
4 Base construction of U-sections 65/40 mm
5 Clamps set in concrete for vertical mullions, all 3.10 m
6 Sash window; the frames consist of two halves which are screwed at the abutments, Neoprene weathering, single glazed
7 Sun protection, plastic vertical blinds, 15 cm wide

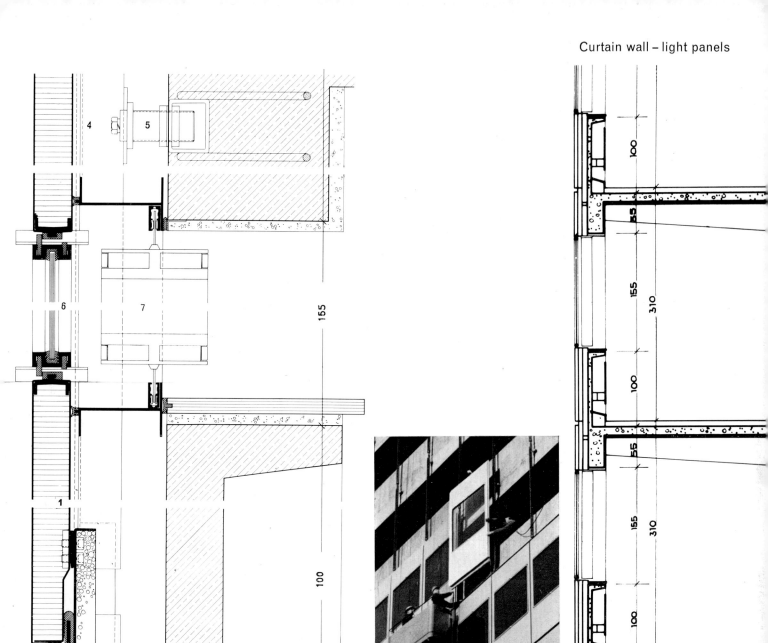

Commercial Bank, Düsseldorf
Architect: Paul Schneider-Esleben, Düsseldorf

Sections 1:50 and 1:5

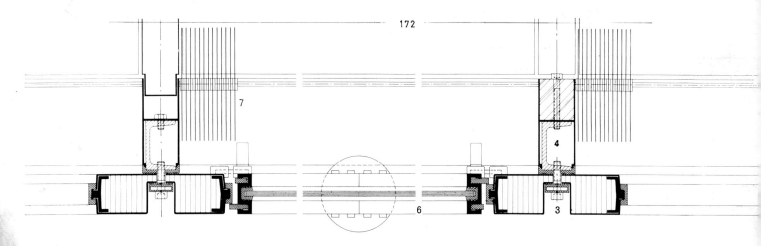

Laboratory building of the Faculty of Medicine, University of Rotterdam, Holland
Architects: S. J. van Embden, J. L. C. Choisy, N. P. H. J. Roorda van Eysinga, H. G. Smelt and J. E. B. Witermans, Delft

The construction of elements and method of assembly are similar to the bank building on the previous two pages. The storey height elements were delivered complete with window ready for assembly. The outer surfaces on both sides are of aluminium coated with a white stove enamelled finish, which is an epoxy resin paint coating fused to the metal at very high temperature. The void space of the panels is filled with polyurethane foam. Fixed pane windows with two panes of insulating glass set in preformed Neoprene membrane sections.
The building has 26 storeys, each seventh floor was designed as an intermediate service floor, appearing on the facade as wide openings (in the photograph they appear below the last completed panel clad storey).

Highrise tower, Westminster, London
Design: Greater London Council
Architects: Sir Hubert Bennett and Sir Roger Walters

The external skin of the storey height cladding panels is made from moulded plastic sheet (glass reinforced unsaturated polyester), 2.3 mm thick. The plastic form is statically grounded.

The skin is poured out with reinforced aerated concrete. Between the plastic and concrete there is a foamed plastic membrane to act as thermal insulation and to compensate for possible movement.

The inside face is of flint and is enclosed by a sheet of plasterboard behind which is a vapour barrier. Because of the light weight it is possible to mount six elements at the same time, which have already been assembled in a steel frame at the factory. The assembly unit, complete with ready glazed window, weighs approx 3000 kg which is an economic weight for the site crane. The size is 823/406 cm and can be transported on the street. The units, over three storeys high, are mounted on the steel frame of the building. The external skin of the element is impregnated with a special resin. Weathering tests indicate it will have a life of at least 20 years. In the event of surface damage the sheets can be re-treated.

The windows, pivot window in aluminium frames, can be turned through 180°. The construction is especially economical for high rise housing because the low surface weight (including windows approx 90 kg/m²) make possible savings in construction and foundations.

Curtain wall – heavy panels

Primary school in Bochum-Harpen and
secondary modern school in Unna-Königsborn, Germany
Architect: Otto Heinz Groth, Dortmund

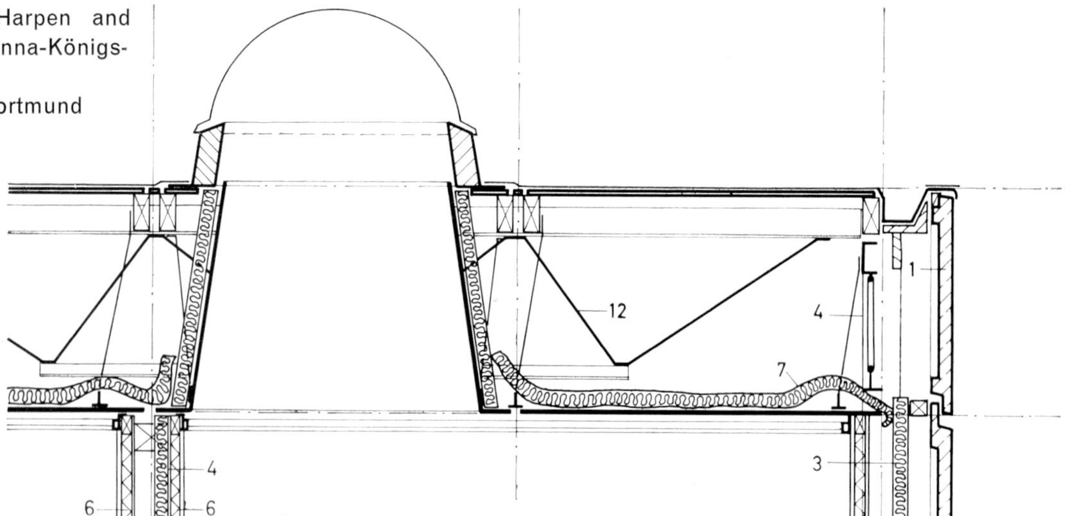

1 Precast concrete component
2 Zinc sheet
3 Insulating mat stitched between bitumen paper
4 Steel column 100/100/8 mm
5 Steel window fixed glazed
6 Precast component: plasterboard, honeycomb
   core, plasterboard
7 Mineral wool
8 Plasterboard sheet
9 Insulating casing
10 Aluminium ceiling section
11 Timber door
12 Light lattice beam
13 Pumice concrete panels
14 Sound reducing sheet
15 Floating screed
16 Sill spandrel, enamelled steel

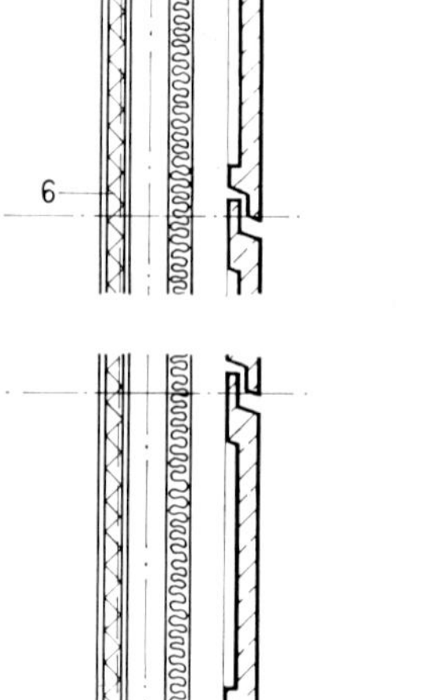

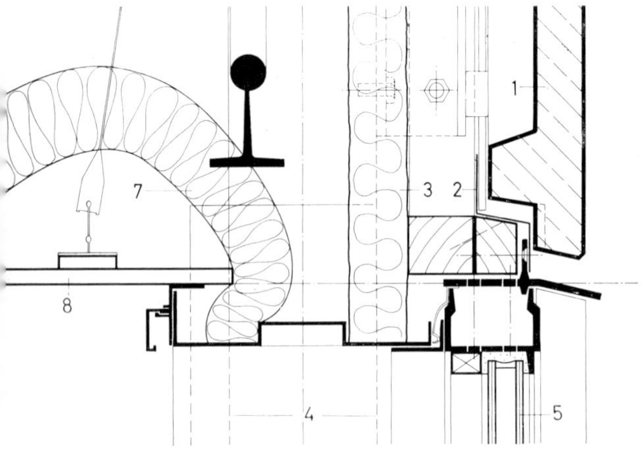

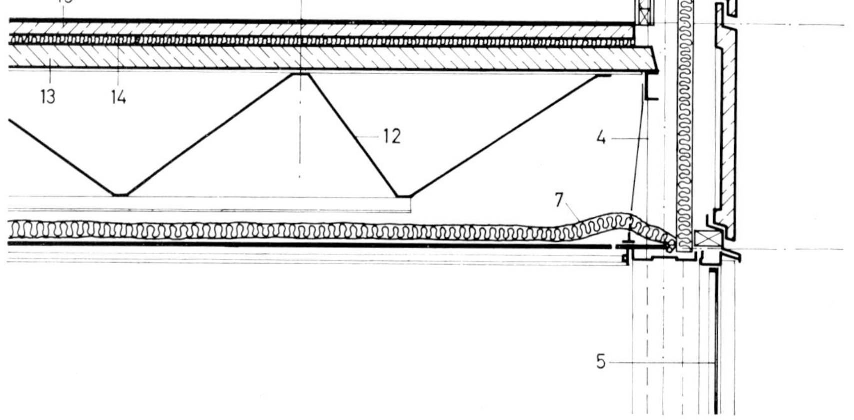

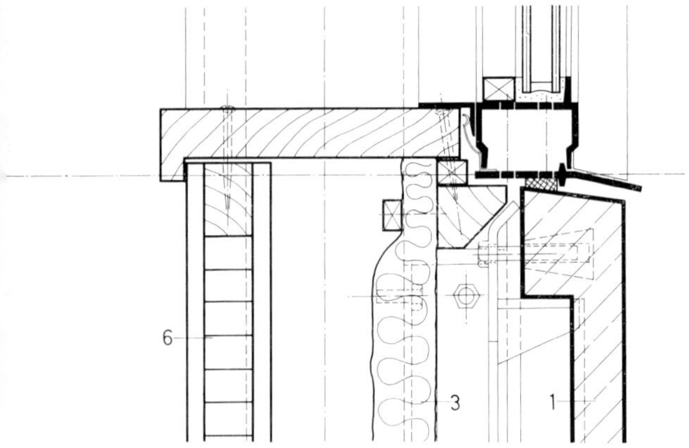

1 : 5

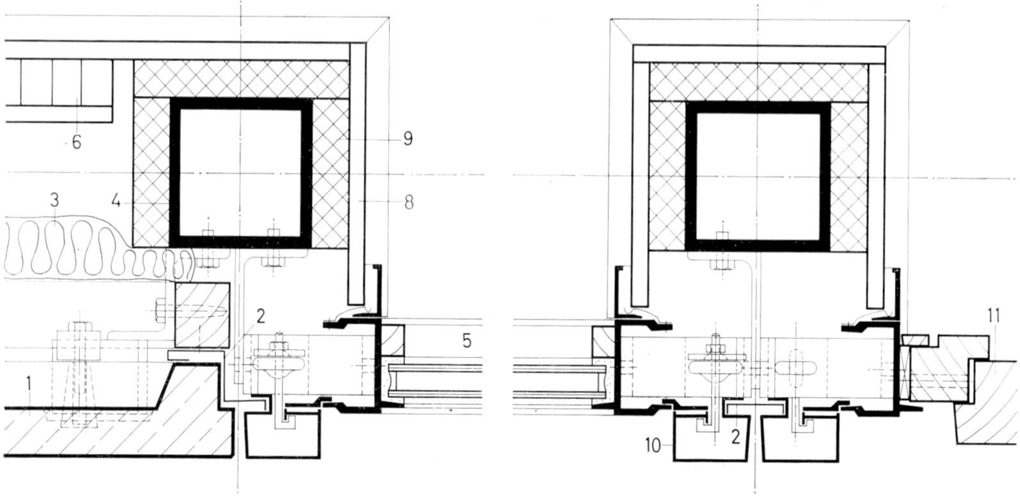

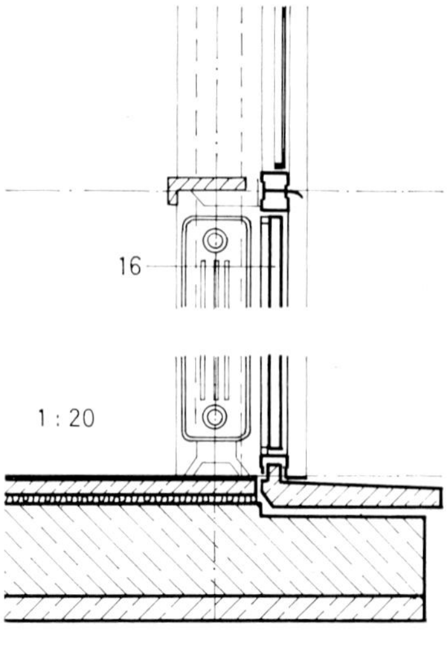

1 : 20

Primary school in Bochum-Harpen (above) and secondary modern school in Unna-Königsborn, Germany
Architect: Otto Heinz Groth, Dortmund

The Brockhouse steel construction system is a method of system building of prefabricated components. Beside the facade elements shown here (exposed aggregate concrete, enamelled steel) there are also timber elements.

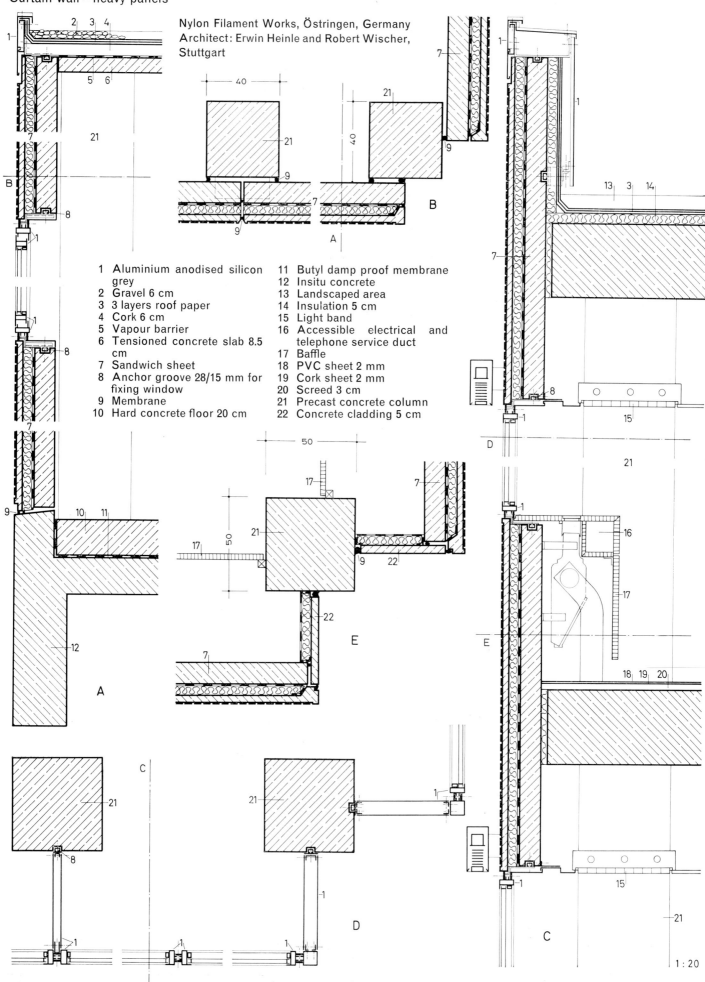

Nylon Filament Works, Östringen, Germany
Architect: Erwin Heinle and Robert Wischer, Stuttgart

1 Aluminium anodised silicon grey
2 Gravel 6 cm
3 3 layers roof paper
4 Cork 6 cm
5 Vapour barrier
6 Tensioned concrete slab 8.5 cm
7 Sandwich sheet
8 Anchor groove 28/15 mm for fixing window
9 Membrane
10 Hard concrete floor 20 cm
11 Butyl damp proof membrane
12 Insitu concrete
13 Landscaped area
14 Insulation 5 cm
15 Light band
16 Accessible electrical and telephone service duct
17 Baffle
18 PVC sheet 2 mm
19 Cork sheet 2 mm
20 Screed 3 cm
21 Precast concrete column
22 Concrete cladding 5 cm

1 : 20

Factory and Offices of the Nylon Filament Works, Östrigen, Germany
Architects: Erwin Heinle and Robert Wischer, Stuttgart, in collaboration with Murray Church, Siegfried Steiger and Alfred Kolbitz
Structural engineer: Kuno Boll
Consultant Engineer: Dr Ing Fritz Leonhardt and Dr Ing Wolfhart Andrä, Stuttgart

Construction of the curtain preformed sandwich panel components took place from outside to inside. Ceramic mosaic sheets on 5 cm concrete slabs. Insulation 5 cm. Polyethylene vapour barrier, concrete slab 12 cm. The slabs are 9 m wide (3 areas of 3 m) on the factory building 1 m high, on the offices 1.80 m high.

Offices

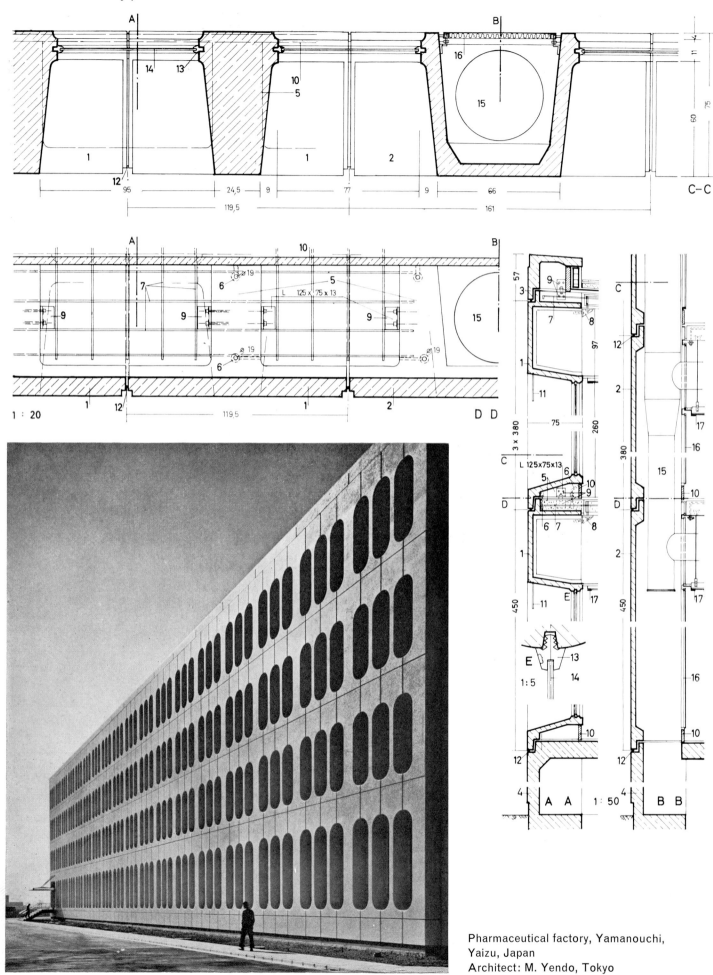

Pharmaceutical factory, Yamanouchi,
Yaizu, Japan
Architect: M. Yendo, Tokyo

left: Pharmaceutical factory, Yamanouchi, Yaizu, Japan
Architect: M. Yendo, Tokyo

The building is the first completed section of a large installation. It is fully air conditioned and fixed glazed. The facade consists of precast concrete components, with the external surfaces spray rendered. The components are of storey height. Ground floor 4.50 m, the 3 upper storeys each 3.80 m. The storey cladding was assembled from bottom to top. 1. Placing of the precast component. 2. Screwing up of the clamps (8) under the storey cladding and the angle (9) on the underlying precast component with bolts and nuts. 3. Preformed assembly of the reinforcement (7): ie, the steels running parallel to the storey cladding were inserted and joined with the bars of the cladding edges and ribs (5). 4. Grouting of the troughs (5).

Because of the form of the elements vertical joints appear only in the area of the sills not, as is usual, in the wall surface. In the precast concrete components of the facade (in every third element) lie the vertical air conditioning ducts. Their cross section determines the depth of the elements.

1 Precast concrete component 119.5 cm wide, standard component
2 Precast concrete component 161.0 cm wide, with air conditioning duct
3 Precast concrete component in front of the roof edge
4 Foundation in insitu concrete
5 Centre ribs in the lower and upper space of the precast component
6 Small pipes for ventilating the joints between the ribs
7 Edge reinforcement of the cladding
8 Cramps under the storey cladding for fixing of the facade components, in each case above on the vertical ribs
9 Securing angle on both sides of the ribs
10 Socket of precast concrete
11 Water shed groove
12 Membrane
13 Structure section of Neoprene with inset adhesive strip
14 Heat absorbent glass 8 mm thick
15 Air conditioning duct
16 Steel sheet 3.2 mm, rear side covered with heat absorbing sheets
17 Suspended aluminium cover

1 Precast concrete component 235 cm high, with space foam filled
2 Window 30 cm wide, aluminium frame, 2 pane insulating glass, fixed glazed (Detail D) with ventilation casement (Detail E)
3 Precast concrete component in front of the slab edge, each 226.8 cm wide, 54 cm high
4 Upper edge of precast floor
5 Membrane height

IBM central offices, Madrid
Architect: Miguel Fisac, Madrid

Sun protection facade of precast concrete elements. They are placed on the slab units of each floor.
Above are round steel cast stirrups welded to steel I sections 80, which are fixed to the edge beam. (Compare sections A-A and B-B.) So that the elements do not give the impression of being load bearing, they are staggered from floor to floor.

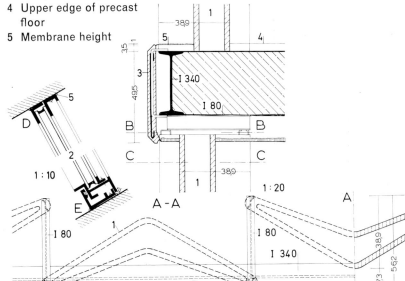

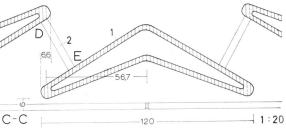

Curtain wall – heavy panels

Postal cheque service and giro counter, Arnhem, Holland

Architects: J. H. van den Broek and J. B. Bakema, Rotterdam

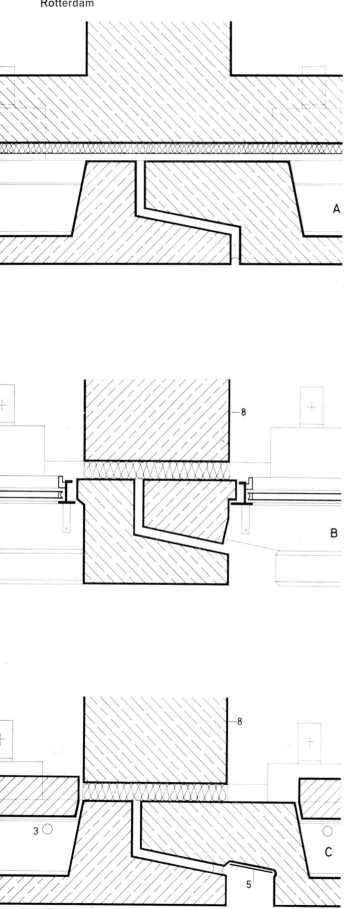

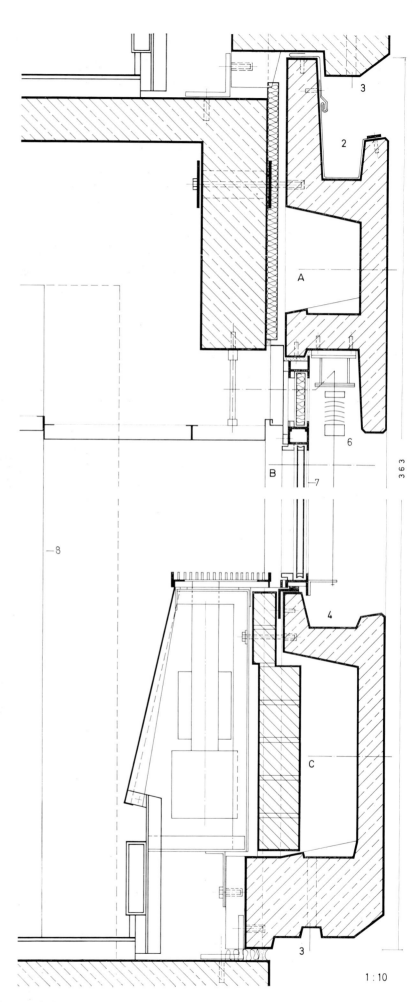

1 : 10

Postal cheque service and giro counter, Arnhem, Holland
Architects: J. H. van den Broek and J. B. Bakema, Rotterdam

1 Precast concrete element, external surface in exposed aggregate concrete
2 Continuous gutter, dressed with copper sheet
3 Plastic pipe for condensation drainage and ventilation of the sill unit
4 Window sill gutter
5 Blue ceramic tiles as water shed for gutters
6 Blind with electric motor
7 Aluminium window, fixed glazed with two pane insulating glass
8 Reinforced concrete column

The concrete elements are 340 cm wide and 363 cm high. They were delivered to the site complete with windows and assembled by site crane without scaffolding. Afterwards the continuous gutter was dressed with copper along the length of the facade as required (detail 2). These gutters also catch the surface water from the windows, and drain the water away individually from each element (detail 4 and 5).

Curtain wall – heavy panels

Department of Housing and Urban Development, Headquarters Building, Washington DC
Architects: Marcel Breuer and Herbert Beckhard, New York, in collaboration with Nolen-Swinburne and Associates

The plan is in the form of a double Y. The photo shows an elevation with car forecourt: all four facades are of similar form. The ground floor lies behind arcades. The support columns are reinforced concrete. The curtain wall concrete cladding elements of the upper storeys are precast. They are mostly 305 cm wide, 365 cm high, and 91.5 cm deep. Window size 193/114.3 cm, casement windows with two pane insulating glass in aluminium frames anodised black. The window aprons are hollow and house the services and air conditioning apparatus; thus the inner surface of the wall is completely flat.

As is seen from the picture, the outer surfaces of the vertical concrete frames of the three lower and two upper storeys are wider than those of the four middle storeys. The window sizes are all the same, so that the facade gives the impression that the lower storeys have a greater load to bear, whilst above the ducts of the air conditioning in the roof are larger.

Detail photograph of a similar construction by Marcel Breuer: a student hostel of the University of New York in Bronx, NY

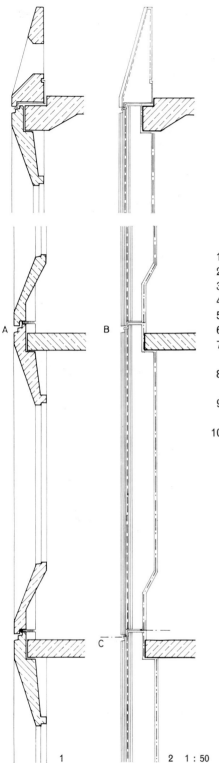

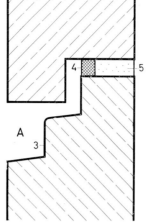

1 : 5

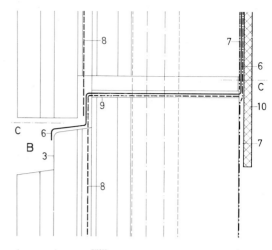

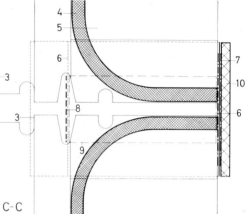

C-C

1 Vertical section through the wall
2 Vertical section through the joint
3 Exposed aggregate concrete element
4 Compressed joint filler
5 Joint mortar
6 Lead flashing 18 cm wide
7 Bitumen vapour barrier 15 cm wide stuck to concrete with bitumen
8 Polythene membrane strips 9 cm wide suspended in joint
9 Polythene membrane strips bedded in cement mortar
10 Polystyrene 12 mm thick, 19 cm wide

1   2   1 : 50

Saint Katharine Dock House, London
Architects: Andrew Renton & Associates, London

This office block takes in the height and mass of the neighbouring early 19th century warehouses. Its exposed concrete columns, with the 1.35 m high light concrete band above them, correspond to the column arcade (compare photograph). The building is clad with precast slabs of exposed aggregate concrete, textured with crushed Firestone. The elements have a storey height dimension of 2.74/4.88 m, or else 1.37/4.12 m. Column grid 5.48 m.

Curtain wall – heavy panels

Hartford Building, San Francisco, California, USA
Architects: Skidmore, Owings & Merrill, San Francisco

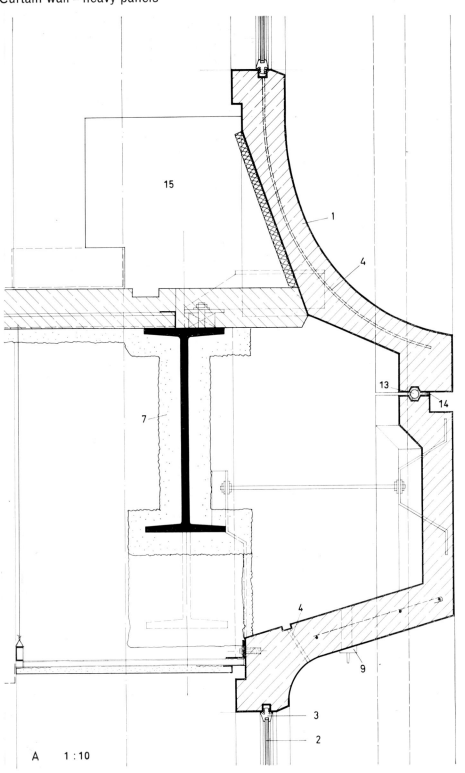

15

1

4

13

14

7

4

9

3

2

A   1:10

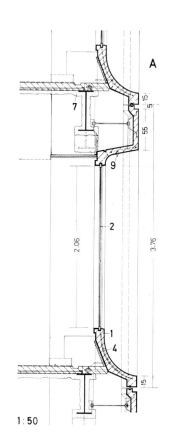

A

7

15

5

55

9

2.06

2

3.76

1

4

15

1:50

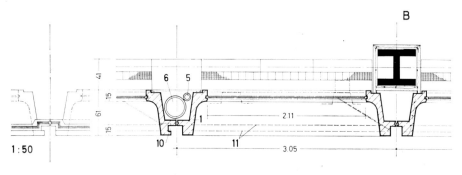

B

41

15

61

15

6   5

1

10   11

2.11

3.05

1:50

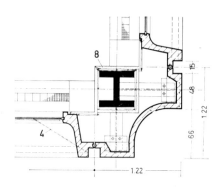

8

15

48

1.22

66

4

1.22

154

Hartford Building, San Francisco, California, USA
Architects: Skidmore, Owings & Merrill, San Francisco

Steel frame construction, 33 storeys, with precast concrete elements
of white exposed concrete

1 Precast concrete element 305 cm wide, 375 cm high
2 Fixed windows, crystal mirror glass, 6-7 mm
3 Neoprene section
4 Plastic condensation pipe
5 Water pipe
6 Air conditioning duct
7 Sprayed asbestos under the ceiling and as coating of the edge
   beam PE 550
8 Fire resistant plaster on metal lathing; column grid 9.15 m (all
   3 elements)
9 Sprinkler installation
10 Guide channel for the window cleaning cradle, both sides of the
   2, 5, 8 and 11 elements. The cradle extends over 3 elements
11 Horizontal abutment of the elements
12 Vertical abutment of the elements
13 Preformed Neoprene joint membrane
14 Mastic
15 Air conditioning apparatus

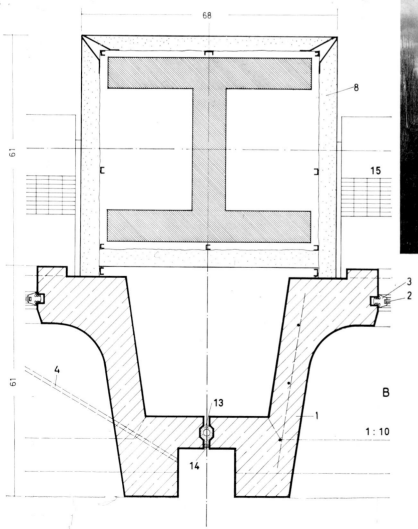

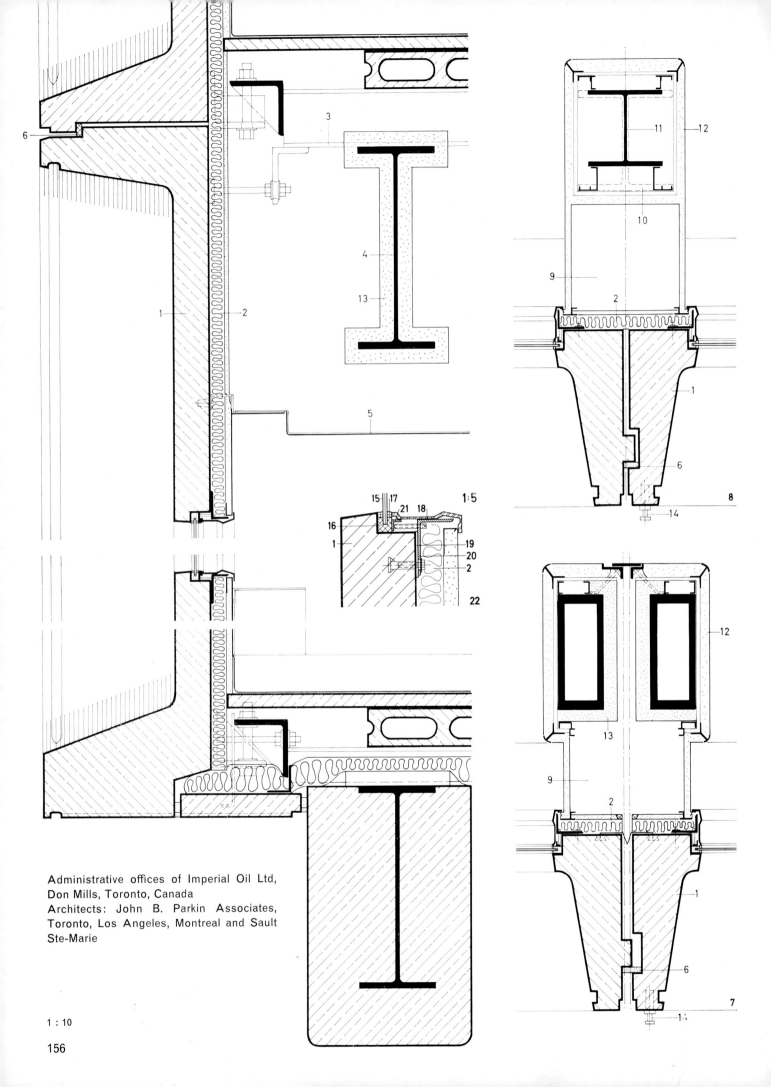

Administrative offices of Imperial Oil Ltd,
Don Mills, Toronto, Canada
Architects: John B. Parkin Associates,
Toronto, Los Angeles, Montreal and Sault
Ste-Marie

1 : 10

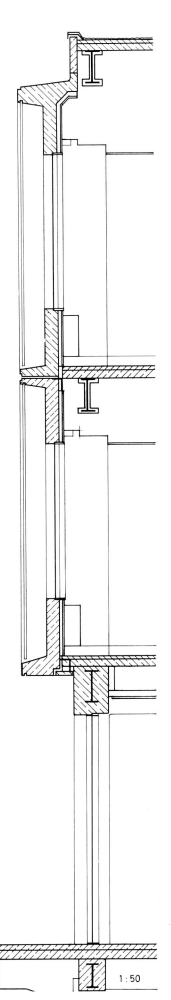

Administrative offices of Imperial Oil Ltd, Don Mills, Toronto, Canada
Architects: John B. Parkin Associates, Toronto, Los Angeles, Montreal and Sault Ste-Marie

Steel frame with concrete slab curtain wall

1 Precast concrete component 1.52 m wide, 3.94 m high
2 Insulation sheet 35 mm
3 Ceiling bearer INP 15
4 Edge beam INP 54
5 Suspended metal ceiling with acoustic sheet
6 Neoprene membrane, joint filling and mastic
7 Horizontal section through the expansion joint
8 Horizontal section through normal joint
9 Service duct
10 Column on first floor IPB 27
11 Column on second floor IPB 20
12 Plaster on casing
13 Sprayed asbestos
14 Fixing bolts for the safety belts of the window cleaners. 5 on each area
15 Mirror glass 6-7 mm
16 Neoprene section
17 Durable mastic
18 Aluminium ceiling section
19 Heat insulation
20 Steel angle 75/50/4 mm
21 Steel angle 13/13/3 mm with adjusting screw
22 Window detail

1 : 50

Curtain wall – heavy panels

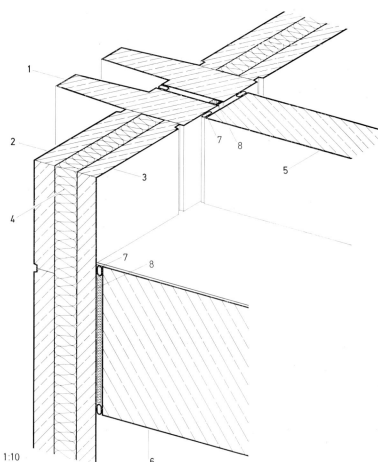

1:10

College of Education and Municipal Sports School, Ludwigsburg, Germany
Architects: Erwin Heinle and Robert Wischer, Stuttgart

The total assembly consists of a teaching wing, sports building, refectory and hostel. The concrete facade elements are in principle the same in all the buildings, lateral struts with trapezoidal cross section, between which are solid or glazed areas, which vary according to the space requirement behind.

All elements are 2.25 m wide; their height varies from 3.73 m = 1 storey up to 13.12 m = 3 storeys. The adjoining drawing shows the basic type which was developed for the teaching wing. Photograph (below right on opposite page) shows an element 9.12 m high, weighing 4200 kg.

Exposed concrete treated externally with silicone and internally with washable, colourless, plastic emulsion. The concrete slabs (4) of the window apron are stuck to the glass wool with an air-dried, bitumen-based mastic adhesive. By this means variable movement of the inner and outer walls can be absorbed. The windows in the teaching wing are installed as reversible units so that the blinds can hang internally or externally.

1 Strut element
2 External skin of cill apron
3 Internal skin of cill apron
4 Glass wool 6 cm
5 Precast concrete internal wall
6 Slab
7 Neoprene tube section
8 Polysulphide sprayed membrane
9 Column
10 Suspension of the facade elements on the edge beam of the roof
11 Fixing of the facade elements on the slabs

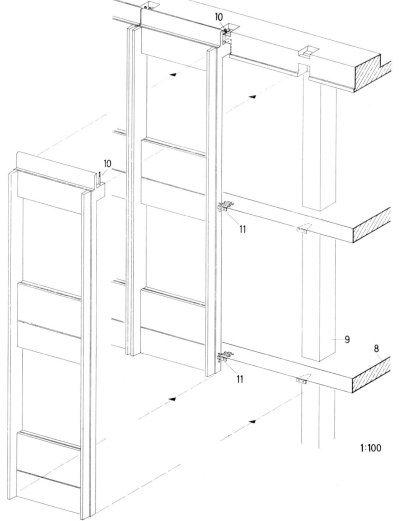

1:100

College of Education and Municipal Sports School, Ludwigsburg, Germany
Architect: Erwin Heinle and Robert Wischer, Stuttgart

above: Gymnasium, below: Teaching wing

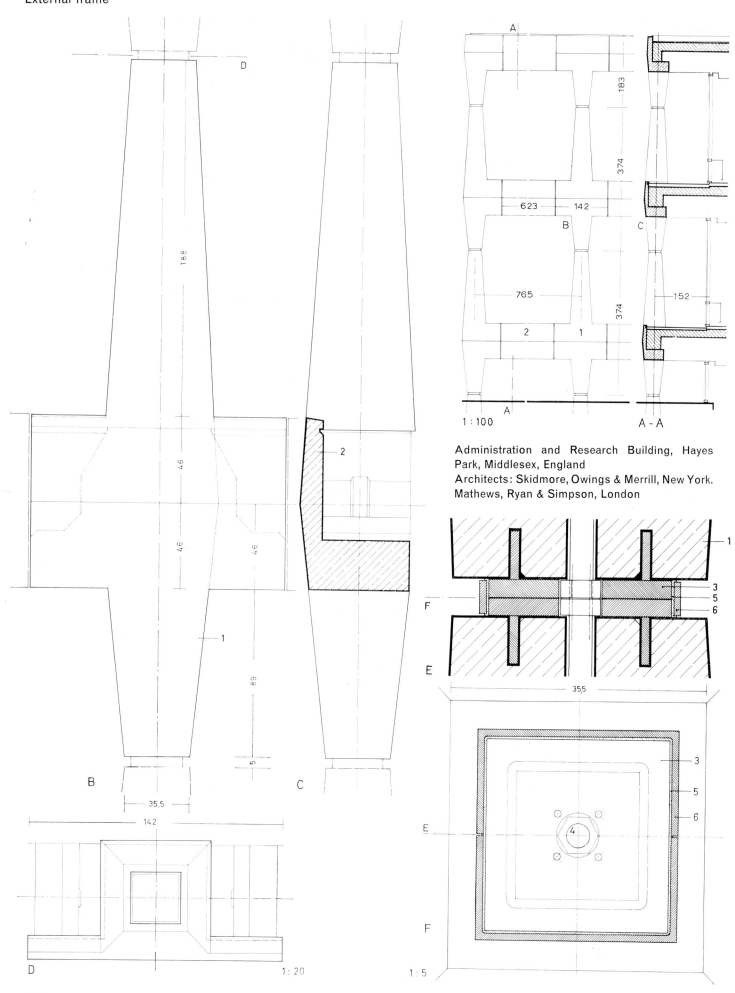

1 : 100

A - A

Administration and Research Building, Hayes Park, Middlesex, England
Architects: Skidmore, Owings & Merrill, New York. Mathews, Ryan & Simpson, London

1 : 20

1 : 5

1 Precast concrete column
2 Precast concrete window apron
3 Steel plate 25.4/25.4 cm 25 mm thick on the upper and lower end of every column with a welded on mounting of flat steel 65/12 mm
4 Round continuity bar at the head of every column
5 Mastic joint filler
6 Enamelled copper cladding

Administration and Research Building, Hayes Park, Middlesex, England
Architects: Skidmore, Owings & Merrill, New York. Mathews, Ryan & Simpson, England

The external surface of the precast concrete component is of exposed aggregate concrete with a granular structure of white Cornish granite set in white Portland cement. The surfaces were saturated with acid and washed off with a powerful water jet. The windows are of aluminium glazed with grey tinted glass.

External frame

Iranian students hostel at the Cité Universitaire, Paris
Architects: André Bloc, M. Foroughi, Claude Parent and H. Ghiai, Paris

Two four-storey buildings are hung in a bearing frame formed of welded steel box sections. They contain the living units. The intermediate floors contain the directorate and the guest rooms.
The steel components are painted black. The external surfaces of the storeys are white and grey Eternit sheets in aluminium sections.

Alcon Building, San Francisco, California, USA
Architects: Skidmore, Owings & Merrill, San Francisco
Construction: Bethlehem Steel Corporation, Chicago, Illinois

The building has 26 storeys. The earthquake resistant, load bearing structure stands approx one metre outside the glass facade. It consists of:

(a) 4 corner posts, L shaped box sections 150/150 cm of steel sheet up to 10 cm thick
(b) 8 columns, cross section 84/84 cm approx grid dimension 15 m
(c) Diagonal bracing box section, whose cross section detaches upwards. Below 46/46 cm out of 7.5 cm sheet steel, above 30.5 cm out of 1 cm steel sheet
(d) Suspended steel sections 6.5/10 cm up to 6.5/30.5 cm. These sheets are always welded at the point of intersection of the diagonal members. Together with storey height members they carry the floors.

The storeys, base surface approx 30/60 m, are freely suspended. Apart from a service core, lifts and staircase enclosure, the office surfaces are completely unsupported.

The frame was assembled for six storeys at any one time (height for a rhomboid) in the following order.

1 Erection of columns
2 Temporary assembly of the floor with timber props
3 Assembly of the diagonals
4 Assembly of the suspended sections
5 Fixing of the floors and suspended sections
6 Removal of the temporary props
7 All steel members are clad in aluminium sheet bronze anodised. Glass wall is of brown tinted insulating glass. Meantime SOM have followed this construction method in the erection of a 335 m high, 100 storey building in Chicago, the John Hancock Center.

Architects

Photographers

Werkfoto Alusuisse 109. Architectural Record, New York 127. Morley Baer, Berkeley/Calif. 155, 163. Otto Benner, Stuttgart 131. Werkfoto Bethlehem Steel 122 (2), 163. Jean Biaugeand, Arcueil/Seine 72 (2). Günther Blunck, Kiel 81. Ernest Braun, San Francisco 79. Brecht-Einzig Ltd., Wimbledon 44 (1), 45 (2), 48 (2), 83 (2). Orlando R. Cabanban, Oakpark/Ill. 56, 57. Casali, Mailand 69. Gabriele Christ, Stuttgart 147 (2). Dearborn-Massar, New York 82. Max Dupain, Sidney 34. Gilles Ehrmann, Paris 162 (2). Foto Engler, Winterthur 109. Jupp Falke, Frankfurt/M. 74. Dieter Geissler jr., Stuttgart 66. Glas- and Spiegel-Manufaktur AG, Schalke 67. Goertz-Bauer, Düsseldorf 51, 140 (2), 141. Gottscho-Schleisner, Jamaica 78. Greater London Council 71, 143 (2). Hannemann, Stuttgart 152. Foto Hatt, Stuttgart 137, 102. Robert Häusser, Mannheim-Kätertal 120. Heidersberger, Wolfsburg 47, 123. Ch. Heilmann 116. Max Hellstern, Regensberg/Schweiz 60. Ib Henriksen, Kopenhagen 46. Werkfoto HPS, Berlin-Burgdorf 117 (2). Foto-Herwig/Aluminium-Walzwerke Singen 62. Werkfoto Hoechst 119. Kurt Hoffmann, Stuttgart 58, 107, 108 (2). A. L. Hunter, Edinburgh 42. S. G. Jackman, Edinburgh 105. Gottfried Jäger, Bielfeld 138, 139. H. R. Jowett, Toronto 157. Foto Kalevi, Makinen 53 (2). Foto Kessler, Berlin 119. S. C. Kroos, Rotterdam 98. Bruno Krupp, Freiburg 54, 135. Werkfoto Krupp, Essen 106. Christian Küenzi, Kilchberg 49. Bill Maris 86 (2). F. Maurer, Zurich 49. Alfred Mehling, Troisdorf 124 (2). Hans-Jürgen Meier-Menzel, Murnau 37, 55. Middendorf, Berlin 115. Michel Moch, Levallois-Perret 59. Barbara Monse, Köln 133. Foto Orgel-Köhne, Berlin 93 (2), 111. Artur Pfau, Mannheim 33, 100. Gottfried Planck, Stuttgart-Botnang 50, 52, 68, 99 (2). Werkfoto Prewi, Winterthur 55. Pius Rast, St. Gallen, 92. Werkfoto B. Rathscheck Söhne, Mayen 89 (2). Walter Rawlings, London 71. Paul A. Rohkst, Rosenheim 76. Inge von der Ropp, Köln 96. Werkfoto Schildkröt-Werke, Mannheim 116. Schmölz-Huth, Köln-Marienburg 61. Schmucker, Gröbenzell 112. Ben Schnall, Hewlett 152. Werkfoto Schöninger Werkstätten, München 101. Shinkenchiku-Sha, Tokyo (Photo Masao Arai) 70, 113. Henk Snoek, London 36, 42, 153. Ezra Stoller, Mamaroneck/N.Y. 73 (2), 126, 161. Hans Guenther Suderow, Hamburg 132. Foto Swiridoff, Schwäbisch Hall 63. E. Thomas, Düsseldorf 104. Friedhelm Thomas, Campione 139. Titzenthaler-Foto, Berlin 130. Romain Urhausen, Dortmund 145. Jan Versnell, Amsterdam 75, 142 (2). Ron Vickers Ltd. 127. J. A. Vrijhof, Rotterdam 94, 151 (1). Hans Wagner, Hannover 41. Peter Walser, Neustadt 2. Colin Westwood, Weybridge 84. Robert Winkler, Stuttgart 125. Michael Wolgensinger, Zurich 91. Heinz Wunnicke, Berlin 67. E. R. Yerbury & Son, Edinburgh 105. Friedrich Zieker, Korntal 159 (3).

Index